THE ULTIMATE GUIDE TO

STRIPED BASS FISHING

THE ULTIMATE GUIDE TO
STRIPED BASS FISHING

Where to Find Them, How to Catch Them

ERIC BURNLEY

The Lyons Press
Guilford, Connecticut
An imprint of The Globe Pequot Press

This book is dedicated to Bob Pond,
the father of modern striped bass conservation.

Contents

Acknowledgments

If I were to acknowledge everyone who helped with this book, I would have to go back sixty years to Mrs. Cora Eppler, who fashioned my first fishing outfit out of a stick, a piece of black sewing thread, and a bent pin, and who then showed me how to roll a dough ball out of white bread and helped me catch my first fish, a small white perch. From that point on, fishing has been a continuing learning process. I have learned that fishing for stripers, or anything else, requires a mind open to new ideas while retaining those things learned in the past and evolving through a combination of the two.

Some of the great anglers I have been privileged to fish with and steal ideas from include the late Kenny Taylor and Russ Wilson. Among the living, I thank Al Ristori, Pete Barrett, Harry Aiken, Claude Bain, Richard Welton, Jimmy Kolb, Doc Trant, Fred Golofaro, and Bob Lick, and also the many others whom I met on the beach, the pier, on head and charter boats, and on the jetties without ever learning their names, or they mine.

I depended on several friends for help with parts of this book that would have been less than accurate without their assistance. Roy Miller was invaluable as a consultant on the biology of striped bass and on fly fishing. Don Avondolio was also very helpful on the subject of fly fishing. Captain Sarah Gardner of Fly Girl Charters helped with fly and light tackle fishing in the sounds behind Hatteras Island. Chris Woodward shared information on southern striper fishing, and Mark Sosin helped with striper fishing in Florida. Ric Burnley helped his old man stay up-to-date on the new stuff.

I depended on several reference books in the writing of this one: *The Striped Bass,* by Nick Karas; *The Fisherman's Ocean,* by David A. Ross; Lefty Kreh's and Mark Sosin's *Practical Fishing Knots,* Tom Melton's *Fishing the Long Island Coast;* and Ken Schultz's *The Fishing Encyclopedia.* I also depended upon the authors of all the thousands of magazine articles I read in *The Fisherman, Salt Water Sportsman, Sport Fishing,* and other publications.

Technical support came from Jerry Gomber at Bimini Bay, Karen Anfinson at Pure Fishing, and Joe Martins at Point Jude Lures.

Neither time nor space permits the listing of everyone who shaped my fishing life and therefore had some input to this book. So if you feel you have helped me along the way, and I am sure you have, but you don't find your name on this page, I apologize and thank you.

Introduction

On a cold October night, a lone surf caster works a beach along the New England shore. He has been casting a Gibbs bottle plug since 2:00 A.M. when the tide began to ebb. Now the first gray light of dawn is just breaking across the eastern sky.

A bit further to the south, a New Jersey jetty jockey has been working a rigged eel from the rocks and has one fish on his stringer. He will fish till 7:00 A.M., then leave for his day job, where his attention will be focused more on plans for tonight's fishing excursion and less on the work at hand.

In Virginia Beach, boats leave Lynnhaven Inlet and aim to be alongside the rock islands of the Chesapeake Bay Bridge Tunnel before the sun is up. Once on site, the anglers will cast surface lures to the junction of the rocks and the bay, where schools of fish have herded bait.

Similar scenes will be repeated from Maine to North Carolina, along the rocky coast of the Pacific, and in freshwater lakes large and small. All of these anglers are after the same fish: the striped bass, a creature that has the ability to stir the emotions of men and women from every economic group and every walk of life.

Some people will spend thousands of dollars in their pursuit of the striper, while others will invest in no more than a simple rod and reel, some bait, and hooks. The truth is, stripers don't much care who catches them or how much they spend on their behalf.

These are democratic fish. They swim close to shore, where even the most poorly equipped angler can catch his dinner. They swim through some of the roughest water on the coast, where anglers need a sturdy boat to reach them. Kids can catch them from a dock, city dwellers can catch them from bridges, and, inland, anglers far from the sea can catch freshwater stripers in lakes and impoundments.

The striped bass is pretty much an American fish. There is a small population in Canada, but most of these fish are born and spend their lives inside the three-mile limit governed by the Atlantic States Marine Fisheries Commission. In the 1970s, this commission began to put in place a management plan to bring the striper back from a precipitous decline. By the mid-1980s, when Governor Hughes of Maryland declared a total moratorium on catching or possessing striped bass in his state, the species was on the verge of economic collapse. Several years passed before every state and commonwealth along the coast joined Maryland, as Senator Lincoln Chaffee from Rhode Island was able to pass a bill in Congress in 1984 that required every member of the ASMFC to follow its regulations or suffer the consequences of a federally enforced moratorium.

The recovery of striped bass is one of the few successful chapters in the history of coastal fisheries management. The fishery was reopened in 1989 under strict regulations and has remained tightly regulated ever since. Today, there are more stripers available than at any time in recent memory. The young-of-the-year classes in the Chesapeake Bay continue to be above average, so barring any natural or man-made disaster, we should have stripers available for many years to come. But commercial fishing once again takes a major toll, and only constant vigilance by recreational anglers will conserve the fishery completely.

Like all fish, stripers can seem dumb as a post one day and smarter than a rocket scientist the next. They are also constantly on the move. The successful striper fisherman will have an arsenal of tactics and techniques to call into play in his pursuit of this fish. In the following pages I will attempt to cover many of these techniques so you will have as much information as you need when pursuing stripers. While I have tried to cover everything, there will be new techniques and products on the market before the book comes off the press. That is the nature of fishing, and the prudent angler will use all the resources available to him in order to keep up with the latest trends. Do keep in mind, however, that Charles Church caught his 73-pound striper from a rowboat, using linen line and a knuckle buster reel on a bamboo rod long before most of us were born.

One

The Biology of the Striped Bass

This chapter will not be a doctoral thesis. It is rather a brief but thorough description of the striped bass. This fish is a somewhat complicated species that spends part of its life in fresh water and part in salt water. Between these stages it swims through a lot of brackish water and comes into contact with all sorts of obstacles that impede its progress.

The Beginning

Striped bass are born in fresh or nearly fresh water. The females migrate to these areas from the open ocean every spring along with some of the males, while other, younger males are already there to meet them. Some male fish do not migrate with the females and spend their lives in the estuary where they were born.

Once the eggs are fertilized, the female stripers, along with a significant number of male fish, return to the ocean and begin to migrate north. The eggs will hatch and the fry have a few days of sustenance in their egg sack before they have to get their own food.

At this time it is critical that the young stripers have a good supply of very small or-

ganisms on which to feed. Some years ago, sewage treatment plants along the Chesapeake Bay treated their waste with high amounts of chlorine. This led to some very clean water, but by killing everything, not just the organisms harmful to people, the striper fry had nothing to eat. This problem has since been corrected.

As the stripers grow, the size of their food increases. Fortunately, estuaries have an ample supply of small fish and invertebrates on which the young stripers may feed. Unfortunately for the young stripers, the estuaries have a large supply of predators that feed on them. Very few young-of-the-year get through the first few months of life, but that is why the females lay so many eggs.

In the Chesapeake Bay, where the majority of the Atlantic coastal stock is born, the state of Maryland conducts a young-of-the-year survey. This has been going on since the 1950s and is the standard by which fisheries managers measure the spawning success of stripers. While one or more of the other coastal spawning areas sometimes can experience a good spawn while the Chesapeake Bay has a bad reproductive year, the Chesapeake population is so critical to the migrating stock it will have an effect on all other striper habitats up and down the Atlantic coast.

Stripers spend their first two years in the estuary before moving out to the ocean. At one point, biologists and anglers thought all two-year-old stripers left the estuary, but now we know some may stick around for up to six years. We also thought that all breeding age females spawned every year, but now we know that some do not. If there is one thing you will learn about striped bass, it is that they refuse to be put into a single category. While the vast majority may do the same thing, there will always be some that go against the grain.

Striped bass generally return to the river where they were born. However, unlike salmon that are going to their natal stream no matter what, a striper's homing instinct is not as strong. No one knows exactly how the bass select their spawning river, but the females will head for one of these areas every spring.

Early Life

Young stripers spend as much time trying to escape being eaten as they do eating. They will be a part of the food chain all of their lives, but during the first years of life they will be somewhere near the bottom.

I had the unique experience of observing this food chain in operation late on a fall day along the Fourth Island of the Chesapeake Bay Bridge Tunnel out of Virginia Beach, Virginia. While I was fishing, I first noticed two anglers hooked up on some good-sized fish right along the south end of the island. I motored slowly over to get an idea of what they had on and what they were using, when I came upon a large circle of tails sticking out of the water. Upon closer inspection they proved to be bluefish tails, and right below them were hundreds of stripers packed into a tight ball. This defense proved futile, as the blues would pick a striper out of the ball much like a party guest taking shrimp out of a bowl.

Most of the time, a bluefish would bite a striper in half, and one of his companions would swiftly take the remaining part. We quickly broke out spinning outfits, tied on poppers, and began to catch those big blues. Even with three fish on at once, the commotion did not deter the other blues from eating. As we progressed along the island we observed at least three more schools of bluefish feeding on stripers. The blues were in the 15-pound class, and the stripers were between 18 and 24 inches. I have seen a lot of interesting things in my 55 years of fishing, but not before or since have I observed anything like we saw that day.

There has been considerable attention paid to the availability of food for the young stripers in the Chesapeake Bay. The primary target of this concern is the menhaden population and whether or not the industrial processing plant in Reedville, Virginia, has been taking too many of these fish. Some of the young stripers in the Maryland portion of the bay have shown signs of stress brought on by a lack of food, leaving Maryland officials and fishermen looking to Virginia for some relief. Since Virginia is unlikely to provide any help with the menhaden problem, the federal government, in 2005, stepped in and placed a cap on menhaden landings in the Chesapeake. Only time will tell if this action has any effect on the striper health in the bay.

While Maryland and Virginia fight over menhaden, an interesting misrepresentation of the facts occurred concerning the predation of crabs by striped bass. A report on the feeding habits of striped bass stated that stripers ate approximately 73 million juvenile crabs a year. Commercial fishermen immediately jumped on this as the reason for the decline of crabs in the Chesapeake Bay. Further investigation revealed that while stripers do eat 73 million juvenile crabs, that is but three percent of the total mortality of the crab population. On the other hand, commercial crabbers account for 98 percent of the mortality on mature crabs.

The political process has become the leading predator of striped bass. There are so many people who want to use the striper for so many reasons, including some so-called nonprofits that see the striped bass as a fundraising lightning rod, that management has become more a matter of politics than biology. In the latest twist, the striper is being blamed for the decline in weakfish. Exactly how far this ridiculous concept will go rests in the hands of our elected representatives, with a potentially scary outcome. Stay tuned.

On to the Ocean

Once the stripers leave their natal waters they begin to migrate. The Chesapeake Bay stock will, for the most part, join the coastal migration and move north towards New England. The stripers that were born in the Hudson River move to Long Island Sound and some join the coastal migration, while others stay there. The Roanoke River stock will hang around the sounds behind the Outer Banks. Many of the fish born outside the Chesapeake Bay will join the coastal migration, and some of the Chesapeake stock will stay in the bay.

Stripers born in other locations, such as the Delaware River, also tend to do their own thing. Tagging studies indicate that most do join the coastal migration, a few stay in the upper reaches of the river, and some move to the Chesapeake Bay through the Chesapeake and Delaware Canal.

The coastal migration is composed mainly of female stripers and the larger males. They move north in the summer to waters where forage is plentiful and the water temperature is well within their preference range of 55 to 65 degrees. During this time, fishing pressure shifts to New England, and most of the big stripers are taken along the Massachusetts coast. When the State-Federal Striped Bass Management Plan began in 1976, Massachusetts landed more pounds of striped bass than any other state, while Maryland and Virginia landed many more fish. Another interesting fact is that Massachusetts had a ban on gill nets in the striped bass fishery, so all of those big stripers were caught on hook and line. In fact, the commercial hook and line fishery was a booming business for many anglers from New England to New Jersey until the establishment of bag limits.

The striped bass survives because it is willing to eat a wide variety of prey. While in the ocean, it feeds on any finfish it can catch, along with squid, worms, crabs, and other invertebrates. Most of its feeding is done close to or on the bottom, but stripers will chase bait to the surface, especially in the fall when they are feeding heavily in preparation for winter.

I once cleaned a 24-inch striped bass that was so full of menhaden it had forced all of its internal organs behind its head. The belly was distended with the four menhaden it had eaten, and yet it was still trying to eat more. The menhaden were fresh, so they had been eaten recently, because a striper needs one to three days to digest a meal, depending on water temperature. This took place in the fall, and this striper was apparently trying to stock up for the winter in one feeding frenzy.

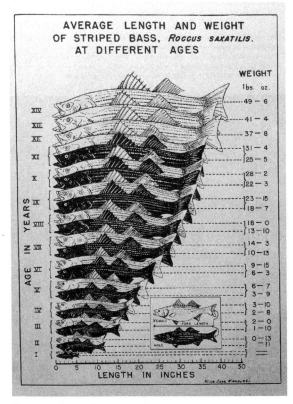

The growth rate for striped bass.

Charlie Whitney, a fixture for many years along the beaches of Cape Cod, once told me a similar story. One of his contemporaries had landed a very large striper in the surf and was going after his buggy so he could put the fish in the cooler. While he was gone, a youngster began picking out the mackerel that were protruding from the striper's mouth. When the angler returned and saw what was going on, he chased the kid away and put all the mackerel back so the striper would weigh more when he sold it at the co-op. Here, too, the striper was so gorged it had fish coming out of its mouth, but still tried to eat more.

Depending on the water temperature and amount of sunlight, stripers will begin their southern migration in the fall. It can begin as early as September in New England and last into December in North Carolina. During this time the fish might follow bait into various rivers and bays, giving anglers some great action. Towards the end of the run, as the water temperature approaches the low 40s, the best fishing will be in the open ocean. Once the water dips below 40 degrees, the stripers stop feeding and hold off the coast of Virginia and North Carolina until spring, when they will once again move towards their spawning grounds.

The Feeding Process

Stripers eat by quickly opening their mouth wide and creating a vacuum, drawing in water and food. They expel the water out their gills and the food goes into the stomach. Their teeth are small, almost like sandpaper, so they don't chop food into pieces like a bluefish.

Stripers will sometimes strike their prey and stun it, then come back and swallow their

Stripers have a large mouth and suck in their food along with a large quantity of water.

line that is used to detect low-frequency sounds. The ears in the head are used to detect high-frequency sounds.

Sound travels much faster in water than it does in the air, so the sound of a nearby prey is the first thing a striper senses. It can be a low frequency sound, like the beating of a tail, or a high frequency sound, such as the splashing of a popper across the surface of the water. This is part of the reason why some lures work better than others: they sound like food to the fish.

A striper's eyes are set alongside its head, and this results in both binocular and monocular vision. There is a blind spot right in front of the fish and along its side and back. A bait placed in the blind spot will spook the fish and make it go away.

The vision a striper does have down its side is monocular, so it cannot judge distance very well until the target moves directly in front, where the fish has binocular vision. This is why a striper will often miss a lure when attacking from the side

A striper will usually feed with its head facing into the current. The water carries information the fish needs to survive; by using

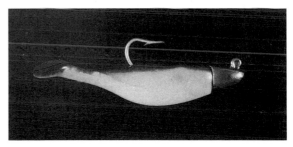

A striper can hear the sound made by the tail of this plastic bait long before he can see the lure.

victim. I have never actually seen that happen, but I have felt this happen when using live bait and with some lures. You feel a tap followed by a take. The two happen so fast I usually don't have time to react to the tap and I pull the bait out of the fish's mouth. Most of the anglers who have reported seeing this happen were live-lining menhaden and saw the striper chase the bait to the surface, stun, and then eat it.

Stripers use their senses to find food. They can see it with their eyes, smell it with their nose, and hear it with their ears and lateral line. The lateral line first alerts a striper to a potential meal. When you clean a striper and remove the skin, you will notice a line of dark meat running down the side of the body. On the skin just above this dark layer is the lateral

the current to move the water past its nose, ears, and lateral line, the striper can gather that information with less effort than it would expend by swimming. This is the process a deer or other mammal would use by facing into the wind instead of running.

The striper has the ability to home in on its prey by sound until it gets close enough to see what's for dinner. At this point the fish can react favorably and eat, or it can react unfavorably and go away. This flight or eat reaction

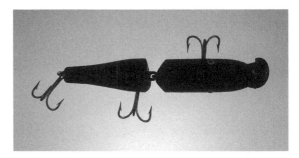

A black lure will stand out very well against a dark sky because a striper has excellent night vision.

Contrast is the most important element when a striper looks for a meal.

may be triggered by the sight of the prey or by the smell. If something does not look or smell right, the striper will either ignore the bait or take off for parts unknown. Remember, stripers, even big ones, still have a built-in defense mechanism that reacts to anything unfamiliar, because strange objects could pose a threat.

The older a striper becomes, the more lazy it gets. Old stripers seldom chase bait across the surface—they wait for the scraps to fall to the bottom. They also won't expend energy pursuing a small bait and will wait for a big bait to gain more protein for their expense of energy. If you want to catch a really big striper, you will have to fish slow and deep with a big bait, because big stripers get that way by eating

large meals that they don't have to work very hard to acquire.

Why should fishermen care how or why a striper eats? Because if you break fishing down to its basics, we are trying to convince a fish to eat something with a hook. Since plastic lures fit with hooks are not part of the striper's regular diet, we have to fool the fish by making it eat something it really does not want. The more we know about the striper's feeding process, the better prepared we are to catch one.

This lure combines sound, flash, and color, all three critical to helping a striper find your bait.

At times catching a striper is so easy it really can't be called a sport. A school of young stripers feeding on baitfish that they have pushed to the surface or cornered behind some structure will hit just about anything that resembles their current prey. On the other hand, getting an old cow to take a big plug or spoon can take a lifetime.

Striped Bass Management

In 1976, I was part of the State-Federal Striped Bass Advisory Panel composed of recreational and commercial fishermen, along with fishery managers from Maine to North Carolina. My position was the recreational fishing representative from Delaware.

At our first meeting in Salisbury, Maryland, we were asked to give our assessment of the primary problem with the striped bass fishery. Everybody knew exactly what was wrong, and, surprisingly, it was always someone else's fault, never our own. The recreational fishermen blamed the commercial guys, the commercial guys blamed the environment, and everyone blamed the government.

In truth, it was everyone's fault. After several years of trying to establish regulations to stop the decline of striped bass, only to have states pay no attention to the problem, Senator Chaffee from Rhode Island introduced a bill in Congress that would impose a federal moratorium on any state that failed to comply with regulations established by the Atlantic States Marine Fishery Commission. In addition, Governor Hughes of Maryland declared a moratorium on the landing of striped bass in his state. Delaware quickly followed suit, and the beginning of the striped bass recovery was underway.

In 1989, the state of Maryland young-of-the-year survey found a large number of stripers at the Hambrooks Bar site, and this specific fishery proved to be so productive that the overall average size was high enough to allow the reopening of the striped bass fishery.

However, the fact that two of the three principle sampling regions were well below the needed average did not matter—the politicians wanted those stripers back in the nets of commercial fishermen and on the lines of charter boat patrons.

Fortunately for the striped bass, regulations were in place to keep over-fishing from occurring, and, finally, in 1993 and 1996, we really did have dominant young-of-the-year classes. These are the 40-inch and larger fish we are now catching, as of this writing, in the spring of 2006.

There have been several more dominant year classes since 1996, and the stock of striped bass in 2005 was as high as it has ever been. There have been many attempts by commercial fishermen, politicians, and some recreational fishing groups to weaken the regulations, but so far they have failed. Currently, the striped bass management plan is written and administered by the Atlantic States Marine Fishery Commission. This is backed by the federal government and requires the states to follow the plan or suffer a moratorium. As with any management plan, some people are unhappy, but for the most part, we go along to get along.

There have also been some misguided attempts to cut the catch. One was the idea that there were not enough big fish in the population during the 1990s, so we must not allow any big stripers to be taken. A little thought will reveal why there were no big stripers. It takes ten to fifteen years for a striper to reach trophy size. In the 1980s, there were no little stripers, so in the 1990s there could not possibly be any big stripers. No need to curtail the catch of big stripers then, because there were not any big stripers to catch. But in recent years, there have been more big stripers showing up all along the coast. As an example the Commonwealth of Virginia has established a new state record striped bass every year since 2004.

Another hot topic is the opening of the Exclusive Economic Zone (EEZ) for striped bass fishing. State-controlled waters run from the coastline out three miles. In locations such as the mouth of the Chesapeake Bay, the state waters begin on the line of demarcation and continue out for three miles. The EEZ extends from the three-mile limit out to 200, and it is controlled by the federal government. After the moratorium began in Maryland, commercial fishermen were still landing striped bass and claiming they were caught in the EEZ. The Maryland legislature passed a law prohibiting the landing of stripers in the state no matter where they were caught, and shortly thereafter the federal government closed the EEZ to striped bass fishing.

With so many stripers currently available, there is a push from some quarters to reopen the EEZ. The state of Massachusetts wants the area open so anglers can fish the EEZ between the state's outlying islands. But opponents fear the coastwide opening of the EEZ will increase the recreational catch to the point that stronger restrictions will be needed.

In this angler's opinion, the EEZ should be open for recreational striped bass fishing. The commercial fisherman is governed by a strictly enforced quota, so where he catches his fish does not matter, given how stripers move around. Keep in mind that the recreational fisherman has a two fish per day limit and a 28-inch minimum size, so he too can only catch so many fish. Why should sport fishers be shut out of federal waters? Right now many recreational fishermen are fishing in the EEZ because they know the odds of being caught are slim. The Coast Guard is charged with enforcement of the ban and they have a few other things to worry about.

Tides, Currents, and Moon Phases

Stripers spend most of their time in tidal water, and even when they move to the spawning grounds, they still feel and respond to the movement of the tides. Along the Atlantic coast the semidiurnal tides change four times a day: two highs and two lows. The movement of the tides varies from one area to another with the highest and lowest tides in the north. The tidal range will vary from fifty feet at the Bay of Fundy to five feet along the southeast coast.

Along the Gulf coast the diurnal tide changes twice a day, one high and one low, and the levels are quite low, somewhere in the range of two feet. The West Coast has what are called mixed tides. They occur four times a day, two highs and two lows, but the levels are not the same. As an example, the first low of the day at midnight may be considerably higher than the next low at noon. The first high at 6:00 A.M. may be higher than the next high at 6:00 P.M. The range of the tide will be five to nine feet with the highest range in the south.

The moon and the sun are the primary causes of tides with all other celestial bodies having a small impact. The gravitational pull of the sun and the moon create a tidal wave on the surface of the water. As the earth rotates this wave moves around the globe creating high and low tides all over the world. During the lunar cycle the highest and lowest tides occur when the moon and the sun are aligned at the new and full moon phases. These are called spring tides. When the moon and sun are at a 90-degree angle to one another the tides move the least, and this is called a neap tide.

The moon also plays a role in fishing other than creating the tides. Most surf fishermen like to work at night during a full moon because the light takes the fire out of the water. This fire is actually created by tiny organisms that glow in the dark and make the lure and line appear to be on fire. I know some surf casters who like to fish the up side of the moon while others prefer to fish the down side. As for me, I fish both sides.

The movement of the tides creates currents. These currents are a bit harder to predict than tides themselves because, while they do follow the tides, the currents run into above- or under-water obstructions. As an example, if you have a shallow bay where the only outlet to the ocean is a narrow inlet, the current will flow in and out of the bay well behind the times of high and low tides at the inlet. The further up the bay from the inlet, the later will be the tide changes from the changes at the inlet. Think about a bottle with a small neck. It takes more time to fill and empty the bottle through the neck than it would if you cut off the top and just poured the water in and out.

These restrictions to the current flow create feeding opportunities for all fish, not just striped bass. Small fish and other food items will move with the current and stripers can take up station to pick off a meal. Most of the time these stations will be outside of the strongest current flow, behind a bridge piling, rock, sandbar, or other structure.

As the tide and current move the fish will change feeding stations. A mud flat on low tide can be a hot fishing spot on the high tide.

The entrance to a creek or gut may not be good on the flood but will be dynamite on the ebb when all sorts of bait wash out to the waiting fish. This constant movement is why every angler must be aware of the tides in the places where he or she plans to fish.

Often this means figuring the tides and current flows on your own. I have fished Indian River Inlet for more than fifty years so I have a pretty good idea when the current flow will change as compared to the tide. Here the current will go slack and change direction about one to one-and-a-half hours after the tide changes. The reason I cannot be more specific is because of the different current flows as the tides move from spring to neap and back again. I do get close enough to be there in time for the changes.

Keeping with Indian River Inlet as an example, in the days of my misspent youth, when I would climb out on the jetty, it was important to be there just as the tide began to fall. During high tide the rocks were covered with water and the waves would wash across the jetty, so I would wait for the water to fall and leave the rocks exposed. As the water level fell I would continue out on the jetty until I could reach the end. The next trick was to move back in as the tide rose without getting trapped on the end. Because the tide would rise and fall before the current would change direction I was able to fish the slack at both ends of the cycle.

My days of jetty hopping are in the past (old bones break easily and heal slowly) and now I fish from the safety of the nice, dry, flat sidewalk. Here, too, the angler should know when the tide and current will change. The current flow in Indian River Inlet is quite strong and it is often impossible to get a bait or lure to the bottom during times of peak current. For this reason I like to fish from the change of tide until slack current. This is when the current flow is slowing down and fishing with a lure is easier. As the water moves in and out of the inlet, it fills and empties Indian River Bay. My family had a camper in a park on White's Creek, a tributary of Indian River Bay, for seventeen years so I had to know the times of high and low water there as well. No tide charts were available for this location so I had to base high- and low-tide times on personal observations. The tides at White's Creek followed the times at the Inlet by about two hours. This meant I had to add two hours to the times of high and low tide at the Inlet to determine the high and low tides at White's Creek.

Using these examples you should be able to figure tides and current flows for anywhere you choose to fish. All it takes is some time and close observations of the water to compute the information you need. Keep in mind that the highest tides and strongest current flows occur a day or two after the full and new moons.

Wind

The wind direction and speed plays a significant role in tidal movement, but it does not change the times of high and low tides. An onshore wind will push more water ashore on high tides and keep more water there on the low while an offshore wind has the opposite effect, blowing out the water on low tide and keeping it lower than normal on the high.

Wind also reacts with the current. A wind blowing against the current flow will create some larger than normal waves, while the wind and the current moving together create a very fast drift or make anchoring a boat much more difficult.

In most situations, having the wind against the current only creates a bumpy ride and some more spray on the boat's windshield. However, at the mouth of an inlet, over a big rip at the mouth of a bay or around heavy underwater structure, the wind working against the current will build some very dangerous waves. Unfortunately, this is just the sort of place where stripers come to feed. This in turn attracts striper fishermen who occasionally attempt to take on more sea than their boat or boating skills can handle.

Such places as Sow and Pigs Reef off of Cuttyhunk, Massachusetts, the rip at the north end of Long Island Sound, Hen and Chicken Shoal off the Delaware coast, and the shoals at the mouth of Oregon Inlet in North Carolina are but a few such locations along the East Coast. Each area has some place where the wind blowing against the current creates hazardous sea conditions and great striper fishing.

As we go along through the explanations of various fishing locations and techniques we will often refer to the best times to fish according to the tides and currents. This is always important and, while there may be the occasional exception to the norm, if you fish by the tides and currents, you will find consistent success.

Water Temperature

According to several water temperature charts, striped bass will avoid water below 50 degrees and above 75 degrees. The same charts list the water temperature range where stripers are most comfortable as 55 to 65 degrees. While I agree on the optimum temperature range, I must disagree with the lower and upper avoidance temperatures. In the fall we catch stripers from Maine to North Carolina until the water temperature reaches 42 degrees. In the summer, Maryland anglers will catch stripers with the Chesapeake Bay water temperature well above 75 degrees. I am sure you could also catch them in Virginia under the same conditions, but they have a closed season in the summer. Along the Southeast and Gulf coasts the water temperature is seldom in the preferred range, but they too catch stripers. Along the Pacific coast around San Francisco the water temperature stays close to the preferred range.

While some of the largest stripers of the season will be caught when the ocean water temperature is in the mid- to lower 40s, the stripers caught during the summer when the water temperature is above 70 degrees are generally small. Apparently, big stripers like cold water, and state and world records are, for the most part, caught when the water temperature is in the bottom of the striper's range. The small stripers are much more likely to stay in the bays or rivers where they were born and must tolerate the warmer water in the summer.

While stripers will feed actively in the fall when the water is in the low 40s, they don't do the same in the spring. I have found that the water temperature must go above 50 degrees before we see any consistent action. Fishing will continue to improve until the water hits 60 to 65 degrees, and then the big fish will move on. As with everything having to do with striped bass, this is not carved in stone. There will be fish caught in the spring from 40-degree water, and big fish will be caught in the summer in water like warm soup. These are the exceptions, however, not the rule.

Two

Methods of Take

There are any number of ways to catch a striper, and so long as it works and is not illegal, any method is fine. You will find people who have it in their minds that catching a striper with natural bait is unfair. This is a bunch of hogwash. There is nothing wrong with using bait, trolling with wire line, or any other technique.

On the other hand, there is nothing wrong with setting a difficult goal for personal satisfaction. I have a goal of catching a 50-pound striper from the surf on a plug. This is my goal, not a format for other anglers who like to fish live eels or soak bunker or clams. I would never criticize another angler about his or her choice of technique.

There are, of course, fishermen who have perfected a technique that works well for them and they criticize anyone who does not do it the way they do. This is just stupid. The complete striper fisherman will try as many techniques as he can to the best of his ability, and, while he may have a favorite, he won't be stupid enough to keep doing it while everyone around him is catching fish by doing something else.

In the following pages I will attempt to present as many of these methods and techniques as possible. All are proven to catch stripers, so pick the ones that make sense for your budget and your approach—from shore or boat—and practice, practice, practice.

Tackle

Before getting into all the various techniques, let's talk tackle. When it comes to striper tackle, cheap is not the way to go. High-quality, sturdy tackle costs good money, and if you try to buy on the cheap, you are going to lose fish. Keep in mind that good tackle will last a long time with proper care, while junk is junk and it won't be around for very long, so you'll spend more money in the long run replacing cheap tackle again and again. This goes for everything from the rod and reel to the snaps and swivels.

When you buy good tackle you are obligated to take care of it. I spray all of my rods and reels with WD-40 after every trip. This gets rid of the salt and protects the tackle from rust and corrosion. Washing off the tackle only removes the salt and does nothing to protect the equipment. Try using WD-40, or a similar product, on your rods and reels, and you will find that they will work better and last longer. I have a pair of 1980 Shakespeare reels that are still working fine after twenty-five years of service and show no signs of rust or corrosion.

Fishing Line

Fishing line is the least expensive part of your fishing tackle, so there is no reason not to get the best. The only thing between you and the fish is the line and your knots. High-quality line makes for stronger knots and always performs better than cheap line.

In today's world there are many types of line to choose for your fishing excursions. The old standby monofilament now comes in many types and colors. The lines that claim to be super tough are usually a bit stiffer than those that claim super castability. If you fish in places with lots of hard structure, the super tough lines may be the best choice. If you use light tackle in open water, the softer line will be easier to cast.

Mono takes a rap for having a lot of stretch. While it does stretch, this is not always a bad thing. If you are trolling and a big fish hits, having some stretch in the line can be a good thing. The same is true when fighting a big fish; a little stretch will act like a shock absorber that keeps you from ripping out the hook.

The braided lines that have become so popular over the past few years offer almost no stretch, a thinner diameter than a mono line of similar pound test, and a high level of sensitivity. They excel when fishing with bait or working a bucktail or other jig, because you can feel the slightest tap of a fish's mouth. When fishing in a strong current, a braided line will go deeper than monofilament because its thin diameter presents less of a profile to the water. In the early years of braided-line development, the stuff had the abrasion resistance of wet toilet paper. In recent years, the braided lines have been treated with protective coatings, and now they hold up reasonably well to contact with rough structure.

One thing to keep in mind when considering braided lines is the rating of your rod. If the rod is rated for 20-pound line and you fill the reel with 40-pound braid, there is a chance the rod will break due to the overload. Of course, the drag setting should not allow this to occur if you set it for 20-, not 40-pound line.

When using braided line, you must be very careful when trying to pull a lure or hook out of a snag. The tendency is to crank down on the drag and put a lot of pressure on the rod. This is a bad idea, especially when using braided line. This line has tremendous strength and is almost impossible to break. The best way to handle a snag is to point the rod tip towards the problem and use the boat to put on the pressure. Under no circumstances should you ever try to pull braided line with your hand. Its thin diameter will cut you like a very sharp knife. Carry a wooden dowel and wrap the line around it. Grab the dowel, not the line to pull the snag loose. I tie a mono shock leader on the tag end of the braided line using an Albright or uni-to-uni knot and this connection will usually give before the braided line parts. This system saves a lot of braided line, and so far it has not failed on a big fish.

Another problem I have discovered with braided line is its tendency to form what I call wind knots when I fish with a spinning reel. This occurs when the bail on the spinning reel closes and traps a strand of line over the face of the reel. As the line winds back on the spool, it covers the ends of the strand, and when you make the next cast, the loop over the reel's face comes off and tangles the surrounding line into a big nasty knot. Often this knot can be undone with a bit of patience, but even when successful, undoing the knot costs valuable fishing time.

My solution is to close the bail by hand. It takes a bit of time to get used to this procedure, but I have reduced my time lost untangling wind knots to zero.

Braided line does not work at all with some of the knots I have been using for years. Most often, I use an Albright knot to attach a shock leader of monofilament line to the end of the braided line. I match the pound test of the monofilament line to that of the braided line. This way I can keep on using my favorite knots and leave the new knots to the young guys. The shock leader can be any length from six inches to long enough to wrap around the reel spool several times, with the tag end going through all the rod guides and falling down to be even with the first guide off the reel also known as the gathering guide. I prefer the latter

in most situations. A longer shock leader will take the abuse from repeated casts and have plenty of line for repeated lure or rig changes. Some surf casters will use a much heavier shock leader when tossing big plugs or sinkers. The power generated when casting this much weight can snap a lighter line.

When filling a reel with braided line, first put on some monofilament as a base. This accomplishes two things: it saves money because braided line is more expensive than mono, and it keeps the braid from spinning on the spool. I also use an Albright knot to connect the mono to the braid.

I recently learned that the Albright knot would not hold when connecting Power Pro to monofilament. This type of braided line is slippery and the knot pulls right out. The uni-to-uni knot will work on the Power Pro line, while the Albright is just fine when using Stren or Spiderwire.

Rods

Just about every rod manufacturer has a line of reasonably priced graphite rods, and this is the type now used by most anglers. You can spend a great deal of money on a custom-built rod, but the ones available right off the shelf are of such high quality these days that custom rods are more for the pleasure of the angler than for the requirements of the fishing situation. Some custom rod builders will put a favorite photo of your spouse, children, or grandchildren on the rod. I have had rods made with the image of a striper embedded in the fore grip; as a gift to a car dealer who sponsored my TV and radio shows, I had one made with the Ford emblem. Some anglers have every rod they own custom made in the same pattern and color scheme.

All of my wire-line rods are custom made because I wanted them short and lightweight, with a heavy action. At the time I had them made, nothing suitable was available from the major rod manufacturers.

A good quality rod will set you back $75 to $150 and up. You can pay a lot less and get a lot less. Most modern rods are made from graphite or a fiberglass-and-graphite mix. Striper rods should have a solid backbone and a medium to heavy action when used to cast most lures and baits. Surf rods used in rough water with heavy sinkers and big baits should have extra-heavy action. I am partial to cork grips and through-the-butt blanks. This setup is very sensitive, especially when combined with a graphite reel seat, and lets you feel soft strikes and taps.

Boat rods should never exceed seven feet while surf rods may reach out to twelve feet. The average surf rod will be somewhere in the nine- to ten-foot range while seven footers are often used from the beach when casting small lures in calm water.

There are some specialty rods that are designed for a specific application. Wire-line rods used around the Chesapeake Bay Bridge Tunnel are usually six feet long and very light because the angler must hold them the entire time he is fishing. On the other hand, bunker-spoon rods are often eight feet or more in length because the spoons swim in an arc and the long rods keep them from meeting.

Rod guides should be able to handle the new braided lines without any damage. Modern materials used in the better rods are capable of this. Wire line has its own problems. Some anglers use roller guides while others trust the carboloy guides to do the job.

Quality rods will be wrapped with thread and coated with a good epoxy sealer. Custom rods offer have fancy wraps that add value and beauty to the product.

High quality rods and reels are the key to striper fishing success.

Reels

There are more reels on the market than ever before, and they run the gamut from el cheapos to high priced, top of the line models. I must admit I never thought I would see the day when a spinning reel would cost more than $600, but that day is here.

Just about every reel manufacturer has a line that falls somewhere between the two extremes. These reels typically cost from $75 to $200 and will fill the needs of just about every fishing situation.

You will need several rod and reel combinations to meet the various situations encountered by striper fishermen. Even if you only fish from the surf, you will need a rod and reel for casting heavy baits and another for lighter lures, and still another for working a jetty. Want to have fun with schoolies in the wash? That will require yet another rod and reel. Boat fishermen will need outfits for trolling big plugs and spoons, jigging metal lures, drifting eels, casting plugs and bucktails, chumming, and chunking. Not to mention a wire line outfit or two.

When selecting any rod and reel, make sure you will be comfortable while fishing with it. An unbalanced outfit can make for a long day on the water.

Spinning and casting outfits should balance while being held somewhere near the reel seat. Trolling rods should have a good balance when held in the position used when cranking in a fish. Surf rods follow the same basic rule as other casting outfits, but the balance is even more critical because the rod and reel are heavier and you will be casting and holding them quite a bit during a typical fishing day.

None of us wants to spend more money than necessary, and buying tackle in a big-box store is usually less expensive than buying the same item from the local tackle shop. The problem with big-box stores is the guy in sporting goods today was probably in ladies underwear yesterday. He does not know a spinning reel from a spinning top, let alone how to put together a balanced outfit for striper fishing.

On the other hand, the guy in the tackle shop has never been in ladies underwear, at least not as far as we know. He does know what type of tackle is the best for any type of striper fishing, and he can service the product after the sale. As an added bonus, when you become his customer, he will be more likely to pass along good fishing information that can help you catch more and bigger stripers.

The choice between buying a spinning or bait-casting reel is often nothing more than personal opinion. Both reels will do the job in most applications equally well.

I prefer to use bait-casting or conventional reels when jigging, bait fishing, or trolling. The revolving spool makes it easier to control the line and feel even the slightest hit. When trolling the fish will take line on the strike, and spinning reels with their fixed spool tend to twist the line as it comes off.

Bait casters also have the ability to cast a lure or bait farther than a spinning reel. The revolving spool lends energy to the cast while the fixed spool on a spinning reel only adds friction to the line as it comes during the cast. Of course, bait casters also have the ability to backlash. The newest reels on the market have anti-backlash features that help the angler control the cast, but even the best of these mechanisms can be defeated by those of us who are mechanically challenged.

Spinning reels are fantastic when casting light lures or baits. I use them exclusively when tossing surface or shallow swimming plugs. Both of those approaches call for light tackle and I find that using the fixed spool reel is easier than trying to cast with a conventional. Not that light lures cannot be cast with a bait caster. I covered a few of the BASS Master Classics and watched while one of the pros cast an unweighted worm a good 75 yards with a conventional reel.

The soft plastic baits currently popular in striper fishing are another lure I use with spinning gear. I am far from a bass pro and find the spinning reel works just fine for my unweighted baits.

The drag on any reel must be smooth and able to dissipate heat. As a general rule, conventional reels have a better drag than a spinning reel in the same price range. I know there are some spinning reels in the upper end of the price range with drags that can handle a blue marlin, but I really don't need a $1,000 spinning reel to catch a striper.

In all cases the reel must match the rod. I have seen people using spinning reels on conventional rods and vice versa, forgetting that the spinning reel goes under the rod and the bait caster goes on top of the rod. That might seem elementary, but you'd be surprised how many people I've seen fishing with a mismatch.

When the reel is on the rod the outfit should balance somewhere around the reel seat. A well balanced outfit will be comfortable to hold and cast.

In most applications, a reel that holds 200 to 300 yards of line is more than enough for striper fishing. Do keep the reel full of line as a half full reel is much harder to cast and loses a lot of power when trying to battle a fish.

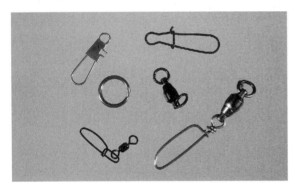

A variety of snaps and connectors. The type in the upper left-hand corner should be avoided.

Connectors

In the past, I always tied my lures directly to the leader, but lately I have started using a small black snap as the terminal connector. It does not seem to deter hits and it does make changing lures much easier and faster. I have used the snap with plugs, bucktails, and plastic shads, all with good success. If you insist on tying the leader directly to the lure, that's fine, and some books suggest that over any other method. But I can vouch for the efficacy of the snap.

The snap or snap swivel is very important. If it is of poor quality, both fish and tackle will be lost. In the case of trolling, the snap swivel keeps the running line from twisting; if it does not do a good job, the line will be ruined.

Once again we will see a wide variety of tackle in this category. The high quality snaps and swivels do not cost much more than the cheap models, but they do a much better job. You want to buy snaps made out of stainless steel or brass and finished in black. Stay away from the safety pin style of snaps because the thin metal clasp that holds the snap together will fail quickly when encountering any type of pressure. Go with cross-loc snaps that won't come apart. As for swivels, get stainless or brass as well.

You can get by with barrel swivels when casting plugs or bucktails, but when trolling any lure or casting with spoons you must use a ball-bearing swivel. While most trolling lures do not spin when working properly, they will spin like dervishes when fouled. Spoons and tubes do spin when working properly. A spinning lure will twist the line into an unruly mess that may end up in the trash.

Personal Equipment

We all like gadgets, and fishermen seem to collect a wide variety of tools and other equipment. Some are absolutely necessary and some are more for our personal enjoyment.

Under the absolutely-necessary category are fishing pliers. Buy a good quality pair and they will last a long time. I am constantly amazed when a reasonably well-equipped angler will pull out a rusty pair of cheap needle-nose pliers and expect to cut a line or remove a hook. Models that have worked for me are the 6½-inch Manley and the stainless steel 6⅜-inch Donnmar model CP850. The Manley pliers are big and heavy so they can handle just about any job from cutting six-pound mono to tightening a lose connection in the fuel line. The Donnmar pliers are much lighter and have replaceable cutting jaws. I have worn out more than one pair of side cutters on Manley pliers and had to buy a new tool because the cutters were not replaceable. Right now I carry the Donnmar pliers on my belt and use them for all my rigging work. I keep the Manley pliers in my tackle box for when I need some brute strength.

Even the best pliers do require some occasional maintenance. Spray them with WD-40 every so often and they will keep right on working.

A new product on the market, the X-Tools pliers, not only float, but the blades will also cut braided line. Right now most anglers carry a pair of pliers to cut mono and a pair of scissors to cut braid.

I also feel a good multi-tool is necessary. I have had a Leatherman tool since they first came out. Currently I have the Wave model, and I use the scissors for cutting braided line. While most of the work in fishing situations can be done with the fishing pliers, having two pairs of pliers is sometimes necessary when removing hooks, or a small knife or screwdriver are handy to fix broken things.

Fingernail clippers are an absolute necessity for clipping the tag-end on knots. But you might want to buy the kind that have a straight clip face, rather then the usual curved face, as that curvature can sometimes allow for the very corner of the clipper to overlap the standing line while you cut the tag, whereas a straight clip face usually doesn't.

A good set of foul weather gear can save the day.

If there is one item that striper fisherman must have, it is a good set of foul weather gear. Stripers like to feed in some pretty nasty weather, and they like to live in places where big seas create lots of spray. Combine all this spray and rain with the cold weather that can come around maximum striper activity, and the need for foul weather gear is obvious.

Gore-Tex is the number-one maker of waterproof clothing, and their products are fantastic. The stuff keeps you dry on the outside and cool on the inside. As good as my Gore-Tex outfit is, I still have a complete set of Grunden bibs and a pullover top. Nothing protects you like solid rubber when the air is freezing and the wind is blowing spray that covers you from head to toe. Top off the outfit with a good pair of rubber boots, and you will be ready for whatever nature has in store.

I have a set of Frogg Toggs that will pack in no space at all and come in very handy in the summer rain. I wear a wide brim hat in the summer to keep the sun off of my ears because they have already suffered some sun damage. I also need a hat to keep the sun from scorching my follicle-challenged head. You'll need a good pair of polarized sunglasses in both summer and winter. Always use sunscreen to protect your skin.

Surf casters, boaters, and especially fly fishermen need an entirely separate list of equipment for their individual disciplines. As we address each type, we will discuss the equipment suited to each.

Three

Casting

Sometimes stripers are close enough that you can simply toss a bait to them. This usually happens when you're fishing from a boat. When you're surf casting, you'll often need to send a plug flying out between the breakers to get on the fish. In this chapter we will look at casting from a boat and tackle surf casting as separate topics.

Casting to Structure

As mentioned earlier, stripers like to feed around all types of structure, and as a general rule they hold tight to stay out of the current. The challenge to the striper fisherman is to figure out not

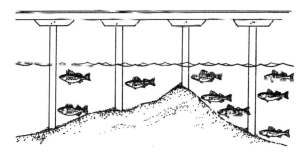

Stripers will stage at several depths along a bridge.

Bridge pilings will hold stripers from one end of the span to the other.

only where the fish are holding, but also how to present a lure to them in a natural manner.

Let's look at bridge pilings, a common structure anywhere stripers are likely to be found. The current will be running from one

21

side of the bridge to the other, creating little eddies around the pilings. Stripers will hold along the lee, or downcurrent, side of the structure waiting for a meal to pass by. In order to make your lure appealing to the striper, it will have to come at him from the upcurrent to the downcurrent side. This requires positioning the boat so the angler can cast the lure to the first piling on the upcurrent side of the bridge and allow the current to carry it past the fish. With the boat in this position, the current will try to carry it into the bridge, not a good thing. In most situations where the angler will be fishing along a bridge, the captain will have to stay on the helm and

Try bright tails during the day and dark tails at night.

keep the boat positioned a safe distance from the pilings. I have fished in conditions where the wind and current worked together to keep the boat moving alongside the bridge with minimum work on the captain's part. I have also experienced conditions where the wind and current worked together with big seas in a concentrated effort to smash my boat to pieces against the bridge pilings. In this situation the captain had his hands full.

Most of the time, anglers use some kind of lead head when fishing bridge pilings. A simple red and white bucktail is the standard, but with so many variations on the market it would be impossible to list them all.

A variety of lead head jigs that are effective around bridge pilings.

One of the more interesting variations is the Hyper Striper, invented by Don Churchill from Newport News, Virginia. It employs a lead head with a small spinner blade under its chin. As the lure falls through the water column, the blade spins, adding a bit more sound to attract fish. The tail of the Hyper Striper is wider than most plastic baits and swims with a slow motion that seems to work well on stripers.

A white bucktail with a white plastic tail rigged with 50-pound leader and ready to fish.

The most popular adornment for the red and white bucktail is a white rubber worm. This lure is so effective that many anglers use nothing else. I, on the other hand, must constantly fool with new ideas, so you are likely to find all sorts of rubber or plastic thingies dangling from my bucktails. I do like a bit more motion to my lures than is available from a rubber worm. The Mr. Twister, Mr. Wiffle, Bass Assassin, and any number of other swimming tail baits will all add motion to the bucktail.

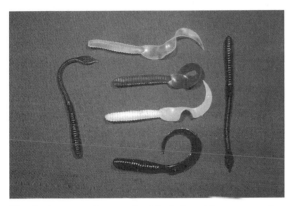

Plastic worms make excellent baits for stripers around bridge pilings.

Plastic shad body lures are also very good for fishing along bridge pilings. I have used Tsunami, Storm, and the Gulp! baits, all with good success.

To work a jig alongside a bridge piling, cast to the leading support and let the lure fall down with the current. As it falls, it is critical for the angler to have control of the lure and be in touch with the line. Quite often the hit is a bit subtle, and unless the angler is in contact with the lure the fish will be lost.

For this reason I prefer a conventional reel, graphite rod, and braided line. Currently I use an Ambassadeur Abu Garcia reel filled with 20-pound Spider Wire on a Berkley Lightning rod for school fish and a BG7000HS Ambassadeur filled with 30-pound Braided Stren on a Fenwick SaltStik rod when hoping for larger stripers. Both outfits allow me to let the line fall naturally with the current while I control the descent with my thumb on the spool. When I feel a strike, I clamp down on the spool with my thumb, set the hook with the rod, and engage the reel, all at the same moment.

A striper will hit a falling jig with only the lightest tap. I have watched as novice anglers missed strike after strike because they did not feel or recognize the tap as a fish. I could see the line jump as the fish hit the jig, while the only reaction from the angler was a request to the captain to please take them to some fish. After a bit of further instruction and a demonstration where I let them watch as the line jumped and I set the hook, most were able to get in on the action. The rest took up golf.

Stripers are likely to hit a jig anywhere from the surface to the bottom, with most of the strikes coming somewhere between. Be prepared for a hit at any time as the jig falls to the bottom. Once it is there, let out a little more line and bounce the jig on the bottom until the pull of the current against the line no longer allows the lure to hit bottom. At this point, engage the reel and slowly work the jig back to the boat until it can be seen just under the surface. Let it hang there for a few seconds before lifting it out of the water, just in case a striper has followed it up to the top.

There will be times and places where the current will be too strong and the water too deep to effectively fish the pilings. Even a heavy jig will be swept away before it can reach the strike zone. Under these conditions, you might have to wait until the current slows before trying to fish. The current will begin to slow after the time of tide change and will continue to do so until the current changes direction. There is also less current flow during the quarter moon.

For reasons known only to the stripers, they will pick one piling over all the others and stage there for a tide. They will probably pick another piling on the next tide, or they may go back to the same one. So the angler should not spend too much time fishing any one piling. Keep moving until you find some action and work that piling until the bite stops.

This striper hit a bucktail jigged along the pilings.

Bridge pilings should produce on the ebb or flood tide. Work the uptide side, no matter the direction of the current flow.

Vertical jigging the pilings is possible. This technique requires a small boat that can work under the bridge and drift very close to the supports. Calm weather and cool nerves are also a requirement.

Begin the drift upcurrent and jig as close to the pilings as possible. This is a very effective method for catching stripers that are holding close to the bottom, as the lure will be in the strike zone the entire drift. Another advantage of jigging under the bridge is the elimination of casting from the equation. Simply drop the jig far enough ahead of the first piling so that

Metal lures are well suited to vertical jigging because they get down quickly.

it will hit the bottom before the boat drifts past. While the aforementioned lures will all work in this application, I have found metal jigs like Stingsilvers, Braids, Yo-Zuri's, and Point Judith lures sink faster and hold the bottom better.

Do be very careful when emerging from under the bridge. A boat running close to the structure cannot see another boat under the bridge until its bow is past the pilings, and by then it may be too late to change course. Accidents like this have occurred at the Chesapeake Bay Bridge Tunnel in Virginia, where there are fifteen miles of pilings.

At times, plugs or spoons will work when fishing bridge pilings. A medium diver such as the Rebel WindCheater works about five to seven feet under the surface and will draw stripers out to strike. A deep diving plug would probably work as well, but controlling this lure in a hard-running current close to a structure is nearly impossible. Save the deep divers for trolling.

A spoon may be let back in the current close to a piling and allowed to swim there, enticing a striper to eat. In most cases, a trolling sinker placed between the leader and the swivel to pull the spoon into the strike zone is the best approach. I like a long leader of at least six feet between the sinker and the spoon. The longer the leader, the less damping the sinker will have on the action of the spoon. The snap swivel must be a ball-bearing model and the leader should be at least 50-pound material. Most spoons, like the Huntington Drone DR 3½, have a ring soldered to the end where the line is attached. Believe it or not, the spoon will work better with the leader tied directly to this ring.

Once the spoon is rigged, just let it back in the current and either jig it up and down or just put the rod in a holder. The current will provide enough action to make the spoon work properly.

Most bridges have lights, and these will attract bait at night. The stripers that move in to eat the bait will stage along the shadow line. They attack when a bait moves close to the line, but they seldom move directly into the light themselves.

Bucktails and small tubes work well in this situation. The approach must be quiet and careful, as any noise, or even a shadow across the water, will spook the bass. The light line can be fished from the bridge, the shore, or from a boat. When using a boat, approach from under the bridge and cast across the light to where the stripers hold. From the bridge, the action is much like vertical jigging, as the lure is gently cast to the fish and worked back to the bridge. Longer casts are required from the shore, but the target remains the same.

Rocks

Rocks come in many shapes and sizes. They can be part of a breakwater, a sea wall, a jetty, a bridge abutment, or a support for a power line; they may be part of a natural line or a single rock jutting above the surface. In all cases, they are powerful fish attractors, providing food and a hiding place—pretty much everything a striper needs to be happy. When the second span of the Chesapeake Bay Bridge Tunnel was built, the contractor set a new group of rocks on the bayside at the north end of the Second Island. The rocks were placed during the summer, and in October I was catching stripers around them.

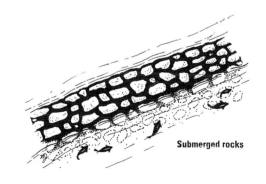

Submerged rocks

Stripers will be tight to the base of rock structure.

An accurate cast to the base of the rocks . . .

In my experience I have found that stripers hold pretty close to rock structure. To catch them, you have to make accurate casts that land the lure at the point where the rocks meet the water. In most situations, actually hitting the rocks is better than falling a foot short of the target. Of course, hitting the rocks is not too good for the lure, and an even longer cast may end up

costing the angler a plug, but stripers want their meal delivered right to their doorstep.

Stripers may feed anywhere in the water column close to rocks. As a general rule, however, they will be close to the surface during periods of low light and move deeper as the light increases. For this reason, cast surface plugs at dawn and dusk and then move to shallow diving plugs as the sun comes up.

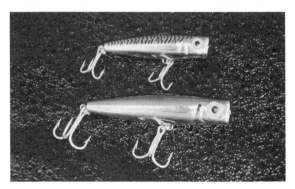

Surface plugs are deadly during early morning and late evening.

Tsunami, Yo-Zuri, Rebel, Storm, and Mann's all make both surface and shallow diving plugs. In all cases, choose a floating plug to prevent it from sinking and becoming lodged in the rocks.

Learning to work a popper properly for stripers will take a bit of practice. I prefer a spinning outfit because it is easy to cast and I can control the action of the plug by working the rod as I retrieve the lure.

Cast to the base of the rocks and let the plug float there for a second or two. If the water under the plug does not explode in that period of time, begin to retrieve the plug by slowly cranking it back to the boat while working the rod tip up and down as fast as possible. This will allow the plug to create

. . . is productive.

plenty of action on the surface, as if it were a wounded baitfish.

A good size striper caught on a surface lure.

When the striper hits a surface plug, avoid the impulse to set the hook. The fish will hook himself, or not; if you miss him, setting the hook will result in having the plug return to the boat through the air and pass close by someone's head.

I once carried two Midwestern bass fishermen on a striper trip, and both would have made Roland Martin proud with their powerful hook sets. The plugs whizzed past my head and landed on the opposite side of the boat. To their credit, those bass fishermen quickly learned not to hook-set surface-striking stripers.

The Zara Spook is another lure brought over to salt water by freshwater anglers. It is worked in jerks by moving the rod tip first to the right and then to the left, with a pause between each motion. This is a much slower action than a popper, and at times it can be very

effective. Keep one handy and give it a chance if your favorite popper fails to produce.

A shallow running plug that floats at rest is a good choice when fishing around rocks.

Once the surface bite is over, it is time to break out the diving plugs. Cast right to the base of the rocks and begin a steady retrieve that is neither fast nor slow. It will take a few casts before you learn the right speed for the particular lure you have chosen, but you don't need any fancy tricks, like putting the rod under water, as another one of my bass fishing clients tried, to catch a striper. I was helping another angler on the boat and was not paying attention to the first guy, so when I turned around and saw he had one of my rods buried almost to the reel seat in the water I was a bit surprised. When asked exactly what he hoped to accomplish by this peculiar technique, he replied he had seen some TV fisherman try it and it worked for him. I explained we were not on TV and please get my rod out of the water and try to behave like a real fisherman.

Rock structures, like bridge pilings, do not hold stripers along every inch of their length. It takes some exploration to find the hot spot for the particular tide and time you are fishing.

Unlike bridge pilings that are uniform from top to bottom, rock structure will have some variations above and below the waterline. A visit to the structure at low tide will reveal some of the outcroppings and holes that may shelter fish on the flood. The remainder of the various underwater structures must be located by fishing experience. If, during the course of your

When the stripers are holding a bit deeper go back to lead heads.

fishing at a particular rock structure, you find action along a certain area, chances are good there is something under the water that is attracting the stripers. In the future give that spot some serious attention, but do not neglect the remainder of the structure, because stripers have been known to be where they should not and not be where they should.

While floating plugs are highly recommended, lead heads will work if the angler can keep them out of the snags. When using a lure that does not float, the retrieve must begin as soon as the lure hits the water, if not before. It is a good idea to close the bail on a spinning reel just before the lure hits the water or stop the cast by putting your thumb on the spool of a conventional reel. Immediately pull the lure away from the rocks, and then allow it to sink while keeping it under control so you can feel it bounce along the bottom. Those who can't chew gum and walk at the same time may find this style of retrieve a bit difficult. The ideal retrieve would allow the lure to sink slowly and bounce along the rocks, but this is very difficult to do, especially when the rocks are covered with grass, mussels, and other marine growth. I have known a few fishermen that were able to pull this off, but, in truth, they did not have any more success than those of us who were using floating plugs.

The new plastic jerk baits will drive stripers nuts when rigged without weight and twitched across the surface. Twitch the rod tip, wait a second or two, and then twitch the rod tip again while retrieving the lure very slowly. This lure works best in low light conditions because it stays close to the surface. That does not mean it won't work during the day, especially when the stripers are chasing bait to the edge of the rocks.

These rocks will be covered at high tide and stripers will use them to ambush bait.

Fishing around a single rock or a scattering of rocks is different than working a single rocky structure, like a jetty. Each single rock is capable of holding stripers, and quite often the fish will be large. As with the rock wall, begin with surface lures, then use a diving plug to root out deep-holding stripers. Because a rock casts a shadow, you can catch stripers close to the surface even in bright light conditions. This does require some very accurate casting, but if the lure can be worked tight to the rock there is a good possibility a striper will intercept it.

A bucktail or similar jig might be worked in here, as stripers will lay tight to the rock while hugging the bottom. This is a favorite trick of big stripers, who find the location a perfect place to ambush large bait. Don't be afraid to try bigger lures, including eel and flounder imitations. The eight-inch or larger plastic shads also work in this situation. There will be the occasional snag, but with a little experience you will learn to keep the jig working just above the bottom.

Rock jetties present a different set of problems. For one thing, they are usually in or very near the surf zone and therefore require some delicate boat handling to prevent a disaster. Jetties are quite often fished at night, further adding to the safety problem.

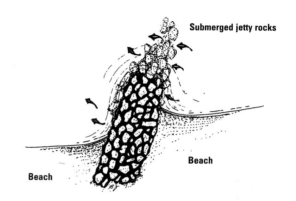

Always work a jetty from one end to the other and both sides when seeking stripers.

Finally, jetty jockeys, who do not look kindly upon boat fishermen invading their territory, will be fishing from many of the jetties you would like to work. A well-placed four-ounce sinker can remove a piece of your gel coat or your scalp, so be sure to give them ample room.

After overcoming all of these obstacles, a jetty is normally fished from the outer end towards the beach. Most jetties have some rocks scattered around the end and may have more rocks littered along the sides. These rocks provide cover for stripers and should be fished thoroughly. Many also lie close to the surface just waiting for the careless angler to pass too close.

The metal-lipped swimming plug is a favorite of anglers working jetties, especially at night. This lure should be retrieved very slowly so that it swims with a side-to-side motion, creating a wake on the surface. The Atom Jr. and the Danny plug are good examples of the metal-lip swimmer. The Bomber Long A and the Cotton Cordell are also sub-surface swimmers that perform well around jetties. Sinking lures should be avoided, because they often end up contributing to the bottom structure.

Birds working over stripers is a welcome sight.

Eel imitations work around jetties during hours of darkness.

Another good lure to use around a jetty at night is any eel imitation. Plastic jerk baits, rigged without weight, will draw stripers like honey draws flies. As with all lures used after dark, black will be the most productive color.

Breaking Fish

Casting to breaking fish is an exciting way to catch stripers. The fish are in the midst of a feeding frenzy and will toss caution to the wind. They often hit anything they can see, if it resembles the prey they are after.

You might think a surface lure would be the best choice for this type of action and often it is, but if the local seagull population has found the feeding stripers, and they usually have, a surface lure is likely to draw strikes from something with feathers, not scales. Removing

a bird from a lure is not the easiest thing to do and usually results in injury, not to the bird, but to the angler.

A variety of metal lures to fit any fishing occasion.

My favorite lure for breaking stripers is a Stingsilver or other metal jig. They cast well and sink fast, reaching the larger stripers often found close to the bottom.

Cast the metal lure as far as possible so that it can be worked back through the school. After it hits bottom, try cranking it back at different speeds until a strike is felt. The change in speed makes the lure stand out against all the real bait and this will attract the striper's attention.

Quite often the strike will come as soon as the lure moves off the bottom. When this occurs, keep the lure working off the bottom for a longer period of time on subsequent casts. I believe stripers will hold close to the bottom waiting for dead or injured bait to drop down. Often these will be larger fish than those feeding right on the surface.

Another way to work the bottom is with a bucktail, plastic shad, or other lead head. In this case the lure should be retrieved very slowly across the bottom all the way back to the boat.

On first sight, one may think a school of breaking stripers would be easy to fish. Just run over to the action and start casting. Unfortunately, this is not always the case. The captain should observe the way the school is moving, the direction and strength of the wind and current, and the position of other boats in the area. Using this information, he should position the boat so the wind and current will push it towards the school without interfering with other anglers. At no time should the captain run the boat through the breaking fish, but I will promise you someone will do just that and spoil the action for everyone.

When this happens, and it will happen unless you are the only boat out there, try jigging a metal lure tight to the bottom, as the fish may have sounded while continuing to feed. Do this until the bite stops or another school appears on the surface. When all else fails, try cruising slowly in the area while looking for fish on the sonar (**So**und **N**avigation **A**nd **R**anging). Most of the other boats will be running around helter-skelter chasing birds, while you quietly bail fish on the bottom.

A good pair of binoculars will help find flocks of birds working over feeding stripers. Concentrate on the horizon, where birds will appear as little dark spots. If your boat has radar it can be tuned to pick up birds and give you the range and bearing of the target.

Early in the fall, most of the birds working over breaking fish will be gulls and turns. As the weather turns colder, gannets will join the flock, and these birds are much easier to see.

Gannets diving in the ocean may signal big stripers feeding below.

They are white with black wing tips and dive from dizzying heights into the water. One word of warning: Gannets do not always work over feeding fish. They dive so deep they can catch bait on their own and do not need the help of stripers to find food.

A rare sight. A lone boat working a flock of diving birds.

While the sight of diving gannets does not always signify stripers feeding on the surface, it does mean there is lots of bait in the area, so the stripers are most likely close by.

Whales are another good sign that the water holds plenty of bait. I have caught stripers very close to feeding whales, sometimes a bit too close for comfort. This is another case of looking for feeding birds and then determining which birds are over stripers and which are over whales.

Feeding birds in general do not always mean stripers below. Shad and herring often draw their own flocks of birds, and this can drive an angler crazy as every lure tossed to the fish is ignored. In this case, try to switch to a shad dart or small spoon, hook a shad or herring, and then live-line it to a big striper that may be following the school. I'll say more on this in the Bait Fishing section.

Most of the stripers caught on the surface under diving birds will be small. It has been my great pleasure to happen upon schools of 36- to 40-inch stripers tearing up the surface, and this is something not soon forgotten. Unfortunately, this is not a common occurrence, but if you follow the preceding instructions, you can make the experience last as long as possible.

Shorelines

Shorelines can be anything from the ocean surf to the shallow quiet of a back bay. Here, the idea is to present the lure in a natural manner as it swims from the shore to the boat.

Let's begin with shallow bays or rivers. The shoreline here may be sand, rocks, grass, or, in some cases, downed timber. Because the water depth is shallow, a stealthy approach is required. I have an electric motor on my tin boat and use it when fishing these areas. The best action here will be during low

light periods, with first light and dusk the optimum times.

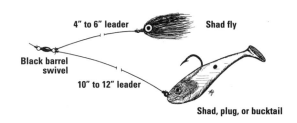

Building a dropper rig.

Stay a good cast away from the shore and place the lure as close to the bank as possible. Allow the lure to sit still for a few seconds before beginning the retrieve. If using a popper, twitch and chug it back to the boat at a fair speed. A swimming plug should be retrieved slowly at a steady pace.

Shorelines are usually sloping beaches, but may be steep banks or cliffs. When the water is deep directly offshore, a bucktail or swim shad may be effective. Allow it to sink to the bottom and swim or hop it on the retrieve. Of course, if the bottom is full of weeds or rocks, a floating plug that dives close to the bottom will be a better choice.

An ideal shoreline is one with lots of vegetation along the banks and a bit of a drop directly offshore. If a ditch or feeder creek empties into the main body of water, so much the better. The drop will not be severe, perhaps a foot or less, but it does give the stripers a place to corner bait. The ditch or creek will hold bait on the flood and empty out on the ebb.

As you navigate down the shoreline, keep a sharp eye out for any disturbance on the surface. It may only be a few ripples or it could be an explosion of bait and stripers, but anything that disturbs the surface requires further investigation. With experience, you will be able to determine the difference between mullet, bunker, silversides, or other common baits by the way they move the water. Fishing a lure that approximates the current bait is a good way to begin.

A selection of plugs to match baits of various size and shape.

For mullet, a long but thin subsurface swimmer is just right, while bunker may be imitated with a deep-body plug. Almost all saltwater lure manufacturers produce mullet and bunker clones. Try a surface lure when no bait is showing. This can be a good prospecting device that will draw strikes from single stripers cruising the shoreline. A new product for saltwater fishing, the spinnerbait, may be a good tool for this purpose.

Creek mouths are prime territory during the ebb tide. Stripers will gather there to ambush bait forced out by the falling water, and you wouldn't go wrong anchoring the boat and fishing with the idea that sooner or later the fish will be by. Many anglers will choose to chum with grass shrimp or clams in this situation in order to give the stripers added incentive. Once the stripers find the chum, cast bucktails, plastic lures, or flies to the hungry fish. I'll say more on chumming in the Bait Fishing section.

Casting along the ocean beach is often effective, but can be a bit tricky. Ocean waves tend to break farther offshore than you might think, and taking a wave amidships can make the night a bit too exciting. Try to position the boat so the angler can cast right up to the beach and then work the lure back through the surf.

Almost any lure type will work in this situation, but I like bucktails and plastic shads. They cast well so the boat can stay farther away from the waves, and they can be worked at all depths, from the bottom to just under the surface. Early morning or late evening can be good times to try a surface popper. Calm nights call for a metal-lip swimmer.

Casting from a boat is the best way to fish along sections of beach that do not provide public access. Because most striper fishing is done during times when the residents are not using the beach, conflicts are rare.

Shallow Water

For our purpose, we will consider anywhere that the depth does not exceed 20 feet as shallow water. Quite often the depth will be much less than that, with stripers frequently taken in three to five feet of water. In recent years, shallow water striper fishing has become very popular in locations from Maine to Virginia. More common in Florida, flats boats are now being used in the shallow bays around New York City, where guides are keeping busy putting anglers on stripers with the most famous skyline in the world as a backdrop.

Not all shallow water striper fishing is done under low-flying helicopters while tractor-trailers whiz past on the New Jersey Turnpike in the distance. Just a few miles east of all this activity is the North Fork of Long Island, where quiet is the norm and big stripers may be taken out of shallow water.

No matter where you fish shallow water, you will need a boat capable of getting you to the fish without running aground. The flats boats used in Florida are great, but expensive. I have a 16-foot Starcraft with a 40-HP Mercury motor and a Minn-Kota Riptide electric trolling motor. This boat will get me into shallow water and the trolling motor moves me along at a quiet pace. It may not be as fast as a flats boat, but I don't go very far.

Two striper fishermen work the shallows in a Florida-style flats boat.

I have heard of shallow water striper fishermen who actually pole their skiffs like Florida guides. At my age, this is not an option, nor do I see the advantage of poling over using an electric motor.

Shallow water striper fishing is more like striper hunting. The fish are usually spooky, and a quiet approach is required. Once spotted, the cast to the fish needs to be perfectly placed, and the retrieve has to be enticing without scaring the fish away.

Good eyesight is important, but knowing what to look for is equally important. As mentioned before, schools of bait will often swim near the surface, and stripers may be nearby. The fish themselves can create wakes on the surface or appear as dark shadows across the bottom. A pair of polarized sunglasses is critical to finding bait and stripers in the shallows. I wear mine even on cloudy days.

In most cases, casts are not made until fish are located. Blind casting may produce a striper but is more likely to spook a fish the angler did not see.

For the most part, bait on the flats will be small. Peanut bunker, silversides, and finger mullet are common, as are crabs, worms, and eels. The lures chosen for shallow water fishing should also be small, not only to imitate the bait, but to make as little commotion as possible when entering the water.

Small bucktails, lead heads with plastic tails, plastic shads, unweighted jerk baits, and plastic worms are just of few of the choices available to shallow water striper fishermen. A light spinning rod and reel do best in these conditions and will cast the light lure with accuracy. Fly fishing is also very popular in shallow water, and we will cover that equipment in a later chapter.

The variety of shallow water found in striper areas is quite extensive. The bottom may be covered with sand, grass, rocks, shells, or any combination of these. Stripers will eat just about anything they can catch, so you may find them chasing mullet on the surface or rooting around the bottom for worms and crabs.

In the spring, when hard crabs are molting, they will hide in the grass until their shells harden. Stripers, and just about everything else that swims, will be attracted to these grass beds in hopes of finding a nice, soft crab dinner. A plastic crab imitation is perfect for this type of fishing, and the ones with a built-in scent, like the Berkley Gulp! peeler crab, are even better. Soaking an unsented lure in peeler oil is not a bad idea. The lure should be rigged weedless and have just enough weight to sink slowly to the bottom. This is one time when blind casting may pay off, because the lure is very light and it is often impossible to spot a striper hidden in the grass.

A fine shallow water striper.

When there are breaks in the bottom grass, work the lure along the edge. I like to let it settle to the bottom, then twitch it across the sand, putting up little puffs as if the crab was struggling to make the safety of the grass bed. When fishing over grass, work the crab just above the tops of the stalks, then let it sink down a bit before bringing it back up. Suspending plugs, like the MirrOlure, will also attract strikes when worked just above the grass.

Open, sandy bottom may not hold very many feeding stripers. They generally prefer to feed around some type of structure, but this does not mean they won't occasionally stop by. Actually, they are more likely to pass through on their way to a more appropriate feeding station.

The good news is that stripers are easy to spot over a sand bottom, and the bad news is that `they are not very comfortable here and are likely to take off at the slightest noise. A surface swimming plug worked very slowly is a good bet, or you might try a very small bucktail or plastic lure bounced along the bottom. Just be sure to cast well past the stripers and work the lure across their path.

A rocky or shell bottom does hold bait and will attract stripers. The feeding fish may be eating small baitfish, worms, crabs, or any number of other things attracted to the uneven bottom. The stripers can be difficult to see if the bottom is composed of dark rocks, but they will stand out over a light-colored shell bottom.

D.O.A. lures are a good choice in shallow water.

In many locations, the bottom will be a combination of various types of structure.

These changes in bottom structure can be good fishing areas and must be carefully explored. Don't be afraid to use small lures to imitate crabs, shrimp, and silversides. These baits are most likely what the stripers are after when feeding in shallow water over all types of bottom structure. The D.O.A. shrimp and the Gulp! crab are excellent lures for this style of fishing.

This striper hit a D.O.A. lure over a rocky bottom.

Shallow water may sometimes be turbid, and spotting fish will be impossible. There may also be some strong currents involved, and where shallow meets deep water, rips will form. Depending on the direction of the current, stripers may be feeding on the shallow side of the rip or on the deep side of the drop. In either case, they will be holding very close to the rip, and the lure must be presented as if it were bait washed to the fish by the current.

Let's assume that you face an incoming current moving from deep to shallow water. The depths might be ten feet on the deep end and three to four feet on the shallow side. Begin the drift on the deep side and allow the

The smooth water to the right is 8 to 10 feet deep while the rip shows where the depth rises to 4 to 5 feet.

boat to move with the current as the lure is cast to the deep side parallel to the rip. The current will carry the lure from deep side to shallows where, at least in theory, the stripers will be waiting. Use a very slow retrieve, keeping just enough pressure on the line to feel the hit. Once the lure has been carried well past the rip, retrieve it to the boat, with the possibility of a strike coming anywhere along the journey. Occasionally you'll have a hit right at

Drifting the shallow side while casting to the deeper water and working the jig back through the rip is the most productive technique.

the boat, either from a striper that has been following the lure or from one who noticed the offering as it left the bottom.

An outgoing current in the same spot would be fished from shallow to deep. Give the lure time to find the bottom before beginning the retrieve. And keep the line tight as the lure falls over the edge, because this is where stripers are likely to intercept it.

The weight of the lead head should be enough to keep it on the bottom. In shallow water rips, this is usually something between one-half and two ounces. At times a spoon will work well in a rip if it can be placed so it flutters in the current, imitating a struggling baitfish. You might also cast shallow water plugs that dive to four or five feet across the current and let the plug swing through the rip with just enough speed from the reel to keep it swimming.

In most cases, a shallow water rip will attract a lot of boats because it is easy to find and does not require a long run across open water. When all these boats operate in shallow water, the noise will have a detrimental effect on the fish. This is not to say they won't feed—they just won't feed as easily as they would without a hundred boats three feet over their heads. The only way to combat this is to get on site as early as possible or fish during the week when the weekend anglers are at work. Just don't anchor in the middle of the rip with dozens of boats drifting around and into your boat.

You can sometimes locate sloughs and holes in an otherwise shallow area. Such structures are usually invisible to the naked eye, unless the water is very clear, but they may be found by drifting or slow trolling over a wide area. I use my electric motor to move over the shallow water while keeping an eye on my sonar for even the slightest difference in bottom depth. When I find a deeper area, I will explore the edges, looking for even deeper water as well as fish. I prospect by casting a bucktail or other jig towards the deepest part of the hole and working it back to the boat.

I won't spend a lot of time in any one location, because the stripers will either be there or not. I may go back to a particular spot several times during a tide, especially if it has produced action in the past. I log any hole or slough I discover into my Garmin handheld GPS.

Four

Trolling

Trolling is the most popular method to catch stripers and is used on most charter and many private boats. The number-one reason that trolling is so popular is because it works. Second, it is not as skill-dependent as casting. If you can let line out from a reel without getting a backlash, you can troll. Finally, trolling covers a large area faster than any other method. This is particularly helpful when seeking stripers in the open ocean or bay.

Trolling Lures

Just about any type of lure will lend itself to trolling. One of the most popular trolling lures is the Mann's Stretch 25, followed closely by the Stretch 30. I have no idea why this particular lure works so well on stripers, but the results are undeniable. I have compared it with

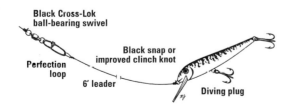

Rig a deep diving plug behind a six-foot leader.

other similar plugs by fishing them alongside one another, and the Stretch always outperforms whatever other lure I am pulling.

Spoons are also popular with striper trollers. The Huntington Drone series, the Arbogast, the Clark, and the Gator spoons will all produce stripers. A special class, known as bunker spoons, does a good job when big stripers are feeding on menhaden.

In recent years, the Mojo rig has gained favor with striper trollers. The Mojo is a heavy lead lure used in place of a sinker to pull the trolled lure down to the level where stripers are feeding. In fact, some Mojos are nothing more than painted trolling sinkers with a hook

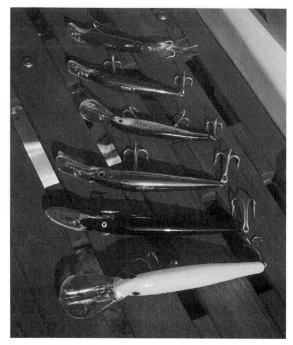

Have a variety of trolling lures on hand to suit any fishing situation.

attached. It is more common to have a large plastic lure attached to the hook on the Mojo.

In shallow water, a bucktail or plastic shad may be trolled. You can also pull a shallow diving plug behind the boat. In fact, you can troll with any lure you like; just remember that some will produce much better than others.

Trolling Tackle

In most trolling situations, the stripers will be in deep water and some weight will be necessary in order to reach them. A heavy weight will put a lot of strain on the rod, not to mention the strike and fight from a large striper. For these reasons the trolling rod must have a stiff backbone that will not collapse under the strain. All the popular rod manufacturers produce a rod that will serve the purpose. While

the top of the line rods are great, I purchased four Shakespeare Sturdy Stik rods in 1989 when I began my charter business and other than several top guides that were destroyed by customers who tried to crank the fish onto the reel, I have not had a single failure. In fact, those rods still look pretty good despite some very rough treatment. I matched the Shakespeare rods with Penn Jigmaster reels and all four of them are still seeing active service.

When selecting a trolling rod and reel combo make sure the two are well matched to one another. The best way to be sure of this is to buy a combo made by the same company and sold as a set. All the major tackle companies have such combos and the only thing you have to do is decide how much you want to pay.

Trolling reels for striper fishing should hold at least 300 yards of 30- to 50-pound line and have the power to crank in big fish. The Penn 330 GTi with a gear ratio of 3.6:1 is a popular choice for striper fishing because it is sturdy and has a level wind that eliminates the need to lay the line on the spool by hand. The Penn 113H with a gear ration of 3.25:1 and the Daiwa Sealine 350H with a gear ratio of 3.7:1 have also cranked a lot of stripers to the boat. Reel manufacturers such as Okuma, Shimano, Abu-Garcia, and others also make models that will serve the striper troller well.

Spinning reels do not perform well when trolling and should be avoided in this application. The fixed spool and bail do not allow the line to play out properly on the strike, and many spinning reels do not have a drag that works as well as the star drag on a conventional reel.

As for line, the braids will get a bit deeper than mono with the same weight rating and an equal amount of weight, but the mono has built-in stretch that absorbs some of the shock from the strike and will cushion the pull on the hook during the fight. In my experience, the mono line will do just fine and is more forgiving to the less experienced angler. When it comes to getting deep, wire line will outdo both mono and braid. We will examine this approach in a separate section.

All trolling lines must be equipped with black ball-bearing snap swivels. Even a plain bucktail will spin under the right conditions, and tubes are designed to spin when operating properly. Spinning lures will twist the line and create quite a mess. Do not troll without a ball-bearing swivel between the lure and the running line.

Plugs

Because the Stretch 25 is a fail-safe lure, it is a good choice to demonstrate how to rig plugs for trolling. The first step is to attach a leader to the plug. Use six feet of 50-pound mono tied directly to the split ring on the plastic lip of the lure. Next, tie a perfection loop on the other end of the leader and attach this to the ball-bearing snap swivel on the tag end of the running line. You may choose to attach the leader to the plug with a snap, but this is unnecessary and uses more tackle than required.

With the boat running as slow as it will go, drop the plug back in the prop wash and begin to let out line. You should have the reel in free spool when placing the plug in the water. A Stretch will float until the diving lip digs into the water, and then it will put considerable pressure on the line. If the reel is engaged, that pressure may pull the rod right out of the unsuspecting angler's hand. Be prepared to let

out line as soon as the lure hits the water, and watch it float back until it reaches the distance you wish to fish behind the boat. At this point, engage the reel and put the rod in a holder.

Generally the best approach calls for fishing one plug 50 yards back and the second one another 50 yards behind the first. This is simply a starting point, not something etched in stone. If action is slow, change the distance on both plugs until you discover what the fish want.

I have found having two deep-running lines in the water is about all I can handle with an eight-foot beam. Charter boats in the Chesapeake Bay and elsewhere will run many more lines, including those on their side planers, and I have seen trailer boat owners try to copy this operation with varied degrees of success. I do have outriggers on my boat and will run two wire lines from these when I have plenty of room to navigate. Otherwise, I just pull two lines and seem to catch a reasonable amount of stripers.

If you pulled nothing else behind your boat but two lines with Stretch 25s, you would catch stripers, but, of course, with fishermen always wanting to try different fish-catching techniques, there are many more ways to troll up a striper.

Spoons and Tubes

Before there were trolling plugs, there were trolling spoons. The first models were made of tin and were trolled on tarred handlines from sailboats. Today, most sailboaters would not allow a live fish on the boat, let alone a tarred line.

Rigging a spoon is a bit different than rigging a plug. The spoon will not sink without help, so a sinker must be placed between the

Big spoons produce big stripers.

running line and the leader. This sinker will have a damping effect on the spoon's action, so it is placed at least 20 feet above the lure. I run mine with 30 feet of leader.

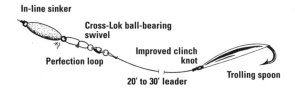

A trolling spoon needs a 20- to 30-foot leader and a trolling sinker.

Tie the 50-pound leader directly to the ring on the spoon and tie a perfection loop in the other end of the leader. Attach the loop to the ball-bearing snap swivel on the trolling sinker. With 30 feet of leader, you will need a leader wheel to store the rig. I make up five or six with different sized and colored spoons before leaving the dock. I put the leader and spoon on the leader spool as soon as it is back in the boat.

Trolling sinkers are shaped like a torpedo and come in weights from less than an ounce to well over a pound. Choose whatever weight is necessary to put the spoon into the feeding zone. Keep in mind there is a point where a lure on mono or braided line will reach its

maximum depth, and the more line you let out past that point the higher in the water column the lure will work. As a general rule, I bounce the sinker three times on the bottom before engaging the reel and putting the rod in a holder. This is not very scientific, but it works.

There is a special class of spoons designed to catch really big stripers when large menhaden are in the area. Called a "bunker spoon" for obvious reasons, this lure requires special tackle and trolling methods to perform properly. A bunker spoon has a great deal of movement from side to side. It can cover eight to ten feet of water and must be set so as not to interfere with the bunker spoon trolled on the other side of the boat. In order to accomplish this, a rod that is at least eight feet long with a relatively parabolic action is used along with rod riggers that set it almost parallel to the water. Very careful boat handling is required to keep the spoons from meeting and becoming engaged.

Bunker spoons require special consideration.

I have never trolled bunker spoons on anything but wire line and would not recommend using mono or braid. The line and leader must be heavy because of the pull from the bunker spoon and the size of the striper you are after.

A 60-pound wire line with a 100-pound leader would not be too heavy in this application. This is no place for light tackle.

Always place a ball-bearing swivel (top) between the running line and the leader when trolling. Barrel swivels (bottom) should only be used when there is no chance that the lure will spin.

Tubes are rigged much like spoons. Tubes are designed to spin, but when you look at one in the water, the head should appear to run straight while the body spins behind.

If you happen to take a new tube out of the package and it swims correctly, go out and buy a lottery ticket, because this is your lucky day. I assume the manufacturer had it right when the tube left his shop, but after traveling to the tackle dealer and being handled by who

Tubes will draw strikes from stripers.

knows how many hands, the newness is all worn out. Adjust the bend in the tube until the proper action is acquired. This is something that takes experience and patience. The first time I saw a charter captain grab a tube, give it a little twist, and put it overboard, where it swam with the perfect movement, I thought, "That was easy." After many attempts to repeat his success on my own boat, I came to realize it was not quite as easy as it looked. The basic idea is to have an elongated S with more bend

These tubes have been formed into the proper shape.

in the tail and a little less in the head. Keep trying; you'll get it sooner or later.

One particular trolling technique employing tubes adds a sandworm to the end of the lure. To my mind this presents the fish with an unusual animal not often found in the wild. Think of a 15- to 36-inch sea creature, the top half made from plastic and the bottom half a large, hairy worm with a hook joining the two halves. I don't know exactly what such a rig is supposed to imitate, but I do know it will catch striped bass.

A smaller version of a tube and worm rig may be cast from the boat or from shore. Use a 12- to 15-inch tube and either a sandworm, small eel, or an imitation of either one. You might have to add an egg sinker to the head of the tube to give the rig a bit more casting weight.

Umbrella Rigs

Umbrella rigs were first used by commercial hook-and-line fishermen who wanted to maximize their time on the water. They would arm every lure on the rig, pulling in as many stripers as possible on each pass. As you might imagine, the number of hooks on each rig quickly escalated to the point where it was quite a task to land a rig full of fish.

Umbrella rigs are striper candy.

The passage of regulations limiting the number of fish allowed per day and the licensing of commercial fishermen brought the arming of each lure to a halt. Today, anglers will only arm the trailing lure, because catch-and-release fishing with an umbrella rig is not a good idea.

An umbrella rig ready for the water.

Pulling from six to twelve lures on a stainless steel umbrella frame with eight to often more than twelve ounces of weight puts quite a bit of pressure on the tackle. A heavy-action rod and at least 50-pound line is the minimum for this technique. A wire line rod and reel with at least 60-pound wire is a common outfit on charter as well as private boats.

In the old days, tubes were the most common lure used on an umbrella rig. Tubes do the job very well and can withstand constant

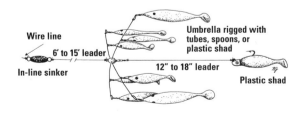

A typical umbrella rig.

use, as well as attacks from bluefish. Tubes imitate a school of sand eels, as this species is common in the striper's northern range. As the popularity of umbrella rigs moved south, different lures were used to imitate the local bait.

Today the plastic shad has become a common armament, and while they do not stand up well to bluefish, because they do not carry hooks, the abuse from stripers is minimal. Color choice is up to the angler, but most begin the day with white, green, or chartreuse. The size of the shad on the umbrella is usually four to six inches, with a ten-inch or larger model used as the armed trailer.

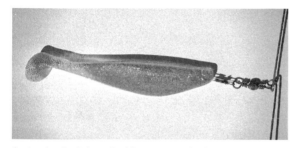

A plastic shad rigged with a snap swivel.

In addition to shads and tubes, I have seen umbrella rigs made with small spoons and unweighted bucktails, and I suspect inventive anglers have employed many other items.

Trailers also vary widely, from bucktails to plugs and everything between. In the Chesa-

Two parachute bucktails rigged with plastic shads.

peake Bay, large parachute rigs are often trailed behind umbrellas armed with plastic shad.

A parachute is a bucktail with the hair tied on backwards so it will pulse when pulled through the water. A parachute will also present a wider profile than a similar size bucktail. Some captains trail one, while others pull two, spaced 12 to 14 inches apart.

An umbrella rig in the water at trolling speed.

Plugs also serve as trailers behind umbrella rigs. The Tomic is a favorite in Virginia, while the Atom Jr. is used further north.

As with just about everything you pull for stripers, an umbrella will require added weight to reach sufficient depth. Since the rig has such a large profile, it will take more weight to sink it than would be required of a single lure. When trolling more than one umbrella rig, you should run them with different weights until the depth where the stripers are feeding is discovered. Most trailer boats will be happy with two umbrellas behind the transom, but because they are a straight-running lure, adventuresome captains may want to push their luck and run three or four. Pray to the fishing gods that they don't become tangled, unless you derive some sick pleasure in untangling such a god-awful mess.

I recommend buying umbrella rigs already set up. Putting small plastic shads on black snap swivels is not my idea of fun, but if you enjoy such things you can save a buck or two by buying the parts and building your own.

Once again you will have to rig the lure on a leader that attaches to a black ball-bearing snap swivel. A 10- to 20-foot leader will be long enough, as there is no worry about damping the action of the lure. In fact, I have spoken with some captains who attach their umbrella rigs directly to the running line, because this removes the process of headlining the leader to the boat. The leader from the umbrella to the trailer will be three to five feet long, with the shorter distance more common. Netting is a bit of a challenge, as the rig will be in the way of the fish on the trailer. Be patient and have the mate pull the rig as far out as possible while keeping the striper in the water.

Storing umbrella rigs can be a problem, because they can become tangled quite easily. One way to keep them apart is to use a large Tupperware container or something similar and sit the rig inside the container. Snap on the cover and, in theory, the rig will be ready to go on the next trip. Do not put more than one rig in each container.

An umbrella rig stored in a plastic bag.

The umbrella should be dry before placing it in the container, and drilling a few drain holes in the container will ensure proper air circulation to prevent mold. The trailers may be stored on leader reels. As a word of warning, your wife may not appreciate you liberating some of her kitchen storage containers, so buy your own at a local kitchenware store, or attend a Tupperware party.

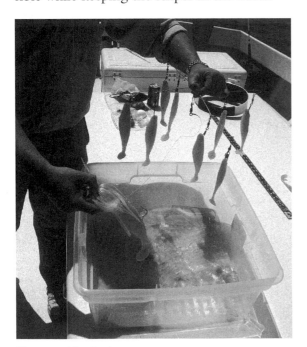

Rigs stored in plastic trays.

Handling a striper on an umbrella rig can be tricky.

Shallow Water Trolling

Trolling in shallow water is not something done every day, but it does have a place in the striper fisherman's arsenal. Such trolling is most common in the spring or fall, when stripers are likely to be in shallow water, and is usually done to locate fish that can then be taken more efficiently by casting.

Because the shallows are usually less than 20 feet deep, use a quiet approach. An electric trolling motor is ideal, but a small outboard will work so long as it is kept at idle speed.

I also find the best results come when the lure is a good distance from the boat. I pull mine at least 50 yards back and will go as far as 100 yards.

Small, shallow-running lures work best in this application. A ¼- to ½-ounce bucktail with or without a plastic or pork rind tail is ideal. A lead head with a plastic tail or even an unweighted plastic lure pulled behind a small trolling sinker will work. I have had good luck with a Tony Accetta 141 spoon pulled behind a ½-ounce trolling sinker. Plastic shads also do well when shallow water trolling. One of the oldest shallow water trolling setups is a Colorado spinner with a sandworm on the trailing hook. A jointed Rebel minnow plug is another good shallow water lure.

This is the place for light tackle trolling. I use an Ambassadeur D6 series reel on a Berkley Lightning rod with 10-pound test mono or 20-pound braided line. While I seldom use spinning tackle for trolling, it is possible to get away with it here.

As always, use a black ball-bearing swivel between the line and leader and keep any trolling sinker at least 24 inches from the lure. Go to 36 inches or longer when pulling spoons.

Don't use any leader heavier than 20-pound test, and fluorocarbon is a good way to go.

While small stripers are the rule in shallow water, some locations, like the Susquehanna Flats at the head of the Chesapeake Bay, can produce some real bruisers in the spring. Large female stripers gather here to spawn, and the state of Maryland allows a catch-and-release fishery. The water is usually far from clear, so finding the fish is a large part of the challenge. Trolling is one solution, if the flats are not too crowded.

Wire Line Trolling

This is one of the most productive methods to catch stripers, and it will work almost anywhere. I have used wire line in water as shallow as 20 feet and as deep as 100.

My first wire line experience came at Shrewsbury Rocks in New Jersey. I was fishing with the late, great Russ Wilson and his son Tommy in Pete Barrett's 20-foot Aquasport that Russ had borrowed for the day. It was the Friday after Thanksgiving, and the weather was cold, but not bitter.

We were on the water at sunrise and had two wire line rigs overboard soon after. Both rigs had umbrellas, and since Russ occasionally sold a few fish and this was long before any bag limits were in place, all the tubes were armed.

The bottom at Shrewsbury Rocks goes up and down like a roller coaster. Russ would run the boat and watch the depth finder, while his son and I were manning the reels. As the bottom would rise, Russ would yell for us to crank in line, and when it dropped, we were told to let line back out. Heaven help us if the rig should ever snag the bottom or not get down quick enough on the drop.

The first strike went to Tommy, and he quickly reeled in a decent fish of 30 inches or so. I was impressed; Russ called it a rat. I got the next turn and was able to bring a similar size striper to the boat. Once again Russ pronounced it a rat as he threw it in the box.

The next hit took drag, and, considering Russ had set it with Channel-Loc pliers, that was quite an accomplishment. Anyone between Russ and the rod would have been trampled to death as he grabbed it from the holder. The fish continued to pull out wire in spite of Russ' efforts to stop her, and you could hear the cash register clicking in his head.

The battle went back and forth for a while, until Russ got the upper hand and started bringing the striper to the boat. At this point, I was ordered to grab the net and get ready to land the biggest striper in the sea.

Unfortunately, that was not to be. The leader to the trailing tube parted and sent Russ backpedaling towards the bow. Once he regained his balance, he stood for just a moment in stunned silence and then burst into the most beautiful, inventive, and long-lasting string of obscenities as I had ever heard.

Once the barrage was over, Russ reeled in the line and discovered a very large striper scale on one of the umbrella tubes and several nicks on the leader to the trailing tube. This set off another blast of cussing and swearing, with particular attention given to Pete, who he blamed for not changing the leader, among other sins, imagined or real.

The rest of the day was anticlimactic. We caught a few big blues that I had to save from Russ, who wanted to beat them to death with the gaff and toss them back. Seems blues are not worth much at the market and they take up valuable time when fishing for the much more valuable striped bass. Not to mention what they do to eels, herring, and other live striper baits.

That was my first trip with Russ, whom I had met that morning. Over the next 20 years or so until his untimely death from cancer, we were to fish together many more times, and each was a story in itself. I miss him to this day. There will never be another Russ Wilson.

Wire line is either single strand or braided. The single strand line is used just about everywhere, with the exception of the Chesapeake Bay Bridge Tunnel, where braided line is used almost exclusively. Both come in various sizes, with something between 50- and 80-pound test most commonly used by recreational fishermen.

Wire line tackle varies as much by geography as by anything else. In the north, where the rod is usually set in a holder, heavy equipment is the norm. In Virginia and other locations where the rod is always held, much lighter tackle is used.

A six-and-a-half-foot rod will work well when trolling from small tin boats, while a seven-footer should be used in larger craft with an eight-foot beam. Suitable models are made by Tsunami, Lamiglass, and Star, just to name a few. Most anglers running wire line will use

Wire line rod on an outroder.

outroders to put as much distance between the lures as possible. This is especially true when pulling bunker spoons.

The wire line rod on the outroder and the mono rod on a flush rod holder.

Bunker spoons require a different style of rod to perform correctly. While the wire line rod used to troll umbrella rigs can have a soft tip and a strong butt, the bunker spoon rod must be parabolic, bending softly in a curve from the butt to the tip. As stated previously, bunker spoons swim from side to side in an arc that may be eight feet wide. It also has a swimming motion that must remain constant. The boat does not maintain a constant speed as it runs

The Penn 320GTI is a good wire line reel.

into or with the seas. Using a parabolic rod will keep constant pressure on the lure by pulling on the spoon when the boat slows and collapsing a bit as the boat regains speed. The eight-foot length helps keep the two spoons apart.

The 330GTi has become the go-to reel for wire line trolling, but the Penn 113H or 114H are also good choices. Penn also makes the 49L, a narrow spool reel that many anglers used for wire line, but I have not seen one in service for many years. The Shimano Tekota has come into fashion with some wire line users and is considerably lighter than most other models.

When you troll this way, don't fill the entire reel with wire. Most anglers use a 100-yard shot on top of a Dacron backing. I use 60-pound Dacron and 60-pound wire.

Connect the single-strand wire line to the backing and to the leader by putting a Haywire twist in the wire and then using an Albright knot to attach the backing and the leader. Most trollers will place a swivel between the line and leader. The swivel can be attached with a Haywire twist.

You will use two types of sinkers when trolling wire line. A trolling or torpedo sinker is usually placed between the wire line and the leader. Some trolling sinkers have a snap swivel on both ends so they can be switched without retying. You can also tie a snap swivel to the line and another one to the leader in order to change sinkers as needed.

A drop sinker or a dipsey, pear, ball, or bank-type sinker can be suspended from a leader tied to one eye of a three-way swivel. The drop leader runs 6 to 18 inches long and is usually made from a line that is weaker than the main line. This will allow the drop leader

A variety of lures that may be trolled on wire line.

to break should the sinker become snagged on the bottom, saving the lure and possibly the fish. Drop sinkers are employed over rocks or other treacherous bottom structure where snags are likely. Anglers also use them ahead of lures when trying to keep the presentation just above the bottom.

Big spoons work well when trolled on wire line.

The length of the leader will depend on the type of lure being used. An umbrella rig will perform well with a short leader or no leader at all. A bunker spoon needs more distance between it and the line. I use a 30-foot leader, but others will go as short as 20 feet.

Single strand wire does have a tendency to kink and braided wire will fray. Both behave very badly if allowed to run without proper supervision. You absolutely must keep all wire under pressure when letting it out and the entire time it is off the reel. Braided wire line will actually backlash, while single strand will become a 100-yard Slinky. Once either happens, the day and the line are pretty much over.

When trolling with wire, an angler must know how much line is in the water. Malin sells premarked single strand wire line or you can mark the line using telephone wire. Telephone wire comes in many colors and is quite thin. You will find it in home improvement stores where it is sold incased in a plastic shield that, once stripped away, will reveal all the small brightly colored wires inside.

Mark the line at 100-, 150-, 200- and 250-foot intervals. First make a barrel wrap with the telephone wire over the fishing wire, and then twist the two wires together as in a Haywire twist and finish with another barrel wrap.

Another way to mark the wire line is with swivels. In the past, black barrel swivels were used, but the new in-line swivels from SPRO and other manufacturers are perfect for this service. Connect these swivels to the wire with a Haywire twist. One advantage to this wire-marking method is that if a section of the wire line is lost or damaged, a new section may be added without replacing the entire 100-yard shot. In most applications where swivels mark wire line, they are set 100 feet apart.

The general theory says that for every 50 feet of line let out, the lure will drop five feet. Add a four-ounce sinker and it will drop 10 feet for every 50 feet of line. Naturally, the strength of the current, the weight and style of the lure and the speed of the boat will all determine in concert exactly how deep the lure will really go. Greater depths can be achieved with heavier sinkers, but sooner or later the water pressure on the line will stop its descent.

Trolling with wire can be a bit of a challenge. If the bottom is flat, the rods may be set in the holder and left alone until a striper hits. In many areas, however, this is not the case because the bottom may drop off or rise quickly, and given that this is the type of structure that attracts stripers, this is where you are likely to fish.

Working over uneven bottom requires cooperation between the captain and the anglers. The captain runs the boat and keeps tabs on the bottom depth, letting the anglers know when to reel up and when to let out line.

Stripers can sometimes stage in one location at the top or behind a piece of structure. In this case, the line is let out until the lure is at the correct depth to make a good presentation to the fish. The captain will make a pass right over the spot and then turn around and come in for another run from the same direction. This sounds easy until several other boats converge on the spot, with everyone jockeying for the same position. If everyone cooperates, a single line will form and all will get a turn.

Special Applications of Wire Line

As mentioned, most wire line trolling is done with the rod in a holder, but there are special applications when the rod is held and the angler controls the lure. These techniques require some amount of stamina from the angler and normally employ a much lighter rod and reel.

Jigging with wire line is the act of moving the rod tip back and forth, imparting a lifelike movement to the lure, usually a bucktail. The parachute-style bucktail is especially good in this application.

The angler will stand along the gunwale with the rod pointed towards the water and move the tip as if he were paddling the boat. The faster the tip moves, the more action in the bucktail, although this is not always the most effective movement. Various speeds should be used until the preference of the local stripers is uncovered. I have a habit of bouncing the sinker on the bottom when jigging. I keep letting out line, controlling the speed with my thumb, until I feel the sinker bounce, and then I stop the line and keep jigging until I can't feel the bottom any longer. In this application I use a dropper sinker about six feet below the three-way swivel.

Jimmy Kolb and the late Kenny Taylor taught the author all about wire line fishing at the Chesapeake Bay Bridge Tunnel.

The two people who taught me how to fish with wire in Virginia at the Chesapeake Bay Bridge Tunnel (CBBT) were Jimmy Kolb and the late Kenny Taylor. They had been commercial hook-and-liners, but most of their catch was weakfish, known as gray trout in Virginia. When the trout disappeared and the stripers came back, the same wire line techniques worked just as well, even if the limit was only two fish per day.

Braided wire is used around the CBBT, along with dropper sinkers in the 12- to 16-ounce range. There are two tunnels along the CBBT and both drop from the surface to about 60 feet in the shipping channel. Stripers love to hang out on the upcurrent side of the rocks and feed on bait washed to them by the current. Most anglers here use wire line to carry a ¼-ounce bucktail with a 7/0 hook down in the current to the waiting fish. In most cases the bucktail will have a pork rind or plastic trailer.

The Bridge Tunnel wire line trolling outfit.

The pass down the tunnel rocks begins at the shallow end, with the boat positioned so the captain can see the upcurrent side of the brick building on the island. Each of the four islands, numbered 1 to 4 from south to north,

has a brick building put there to give wire line anglers a point of reference. The boat's speed is constantly adjusted to maintain the optimum position. If the captain cannot see the upcurrent side or he can see the downcurrent side,

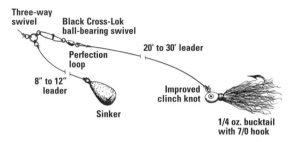

This rig will work over the Chesapeake Bay Bridge Tunnel tubes. It is also effective in open water.

he is in the wrong position, because in either incorrect situation the current will carry the bucktail over the top of the rocks and it will never find bottom or fish. If the captain sees more than 10 percent of the downcurrent side, he will also be out of position and the lure will work too far away from the rocks.

Done correctly, the boat will actually crab along the rip with its bow in the current and its stern at an angle to the rocks. The angler stands in the stern, letting out line until the sinker hits bottom. At this point he will stop the reel with his thumb and bounce the sinker on the rocks until he can no longer feel bottom, at which point he continues to let out more line. Keep the lever that engages the reel close at hand in case the rig becomes snagged on the bottom. It is rare, but a few anglers have had their thumb trapped between the spool and the bridge of the reel as the boat continued to move forward and the line remained tight to the bottom. I understand the feeling is akin to slamming a car door on your thumb.

When the rig does become snagged, and it will, do not turn around and go back in an attempt to free the sinker or bucktail. Keep going forward until something breaks, usually the sinker leader, then reel in, retie, and go back out. Yes, you will lose a lot of sinkers, but turning around on the rip with several boats behind you just to save a couple of bucks will not win you any friends and could cause a much more expensive disaster.

Rig the bucktail on a 30-foot, 50-pound mono leader. Due to its small size and light weight it floats around the rocks like a disoriented baitfish. Stripers find this irresistible and eat the lure with a solid strike.

Now the fun really begins as you engage the reel and the line comes tight. You have a good-sized striper on a short wire line and every shake of his head goes right to your arms. You are also cranking in a big sinker against a strong current and thinking anyone who says wire line is not a sporting way to catch stripers never tried this.

The captain should turn the boat away from the rocks to give you a better chance to fight your fish. He may also choose to keep his course in hopes of hooking up another striper.

It would be a rare day if you were the only boat fishing over the tube. When things get crowded, everyone can still fish if they will stay in line and maintain the same speed. The lures are going almost straight down, so the boats will be able to stay close together without snagging each other's lines.

For whatever reason, someone will try to troll across the rip pulling a Stretch 25 on mono, and foul up the whole works. You will also find other anglers doing other strange things, some of which you have never seen before and may never see again. The worst of this behavior happens on the weekends, when those people who have the money to own a boat but not the brains to pilot one correctly launch their nautical dramas.

Playing Together

Mixing a spread of wire and mono lines requires some careful planning and skillful boat handling. Charter captains often use a system that marks each rod with a number corresponding with a holder on the boat. They may pull up to a dozen lines, mixing wire and mono without a tangle. As an example, let's begin counting from left to right as you face the stern. The first rod will be a mono line used from the top of the cabin. It would be numbered 1. The next rod, probably mono as well, will be mounted from the side of the cabin, and it will be number 2. The gunwale will get three or four rods and the transom will carry at least four, normally all wire lines. The numbering continues down the other side and back up to the top of the cabin.

All of the lines are marked, and the mate knows to stop letting out line when the mark reaches the rod tip. Sinkers and lures are never changed, so each line will be at the same depth and the same distance from the boat every time it is let out. The captain carefully executes turns. This sounds a bit complicated, but once set up, it works very well. Even a well instructed party could let out lines after a fish is landed.

Side Planers

The first side planers I heard about were used in the Great Lakes' salmon fishery. The idea is to put a line out away from the boat and outside of its wake. The side planers are designed to move away from the boat as the water pressure pulls them in that direction. Some will only carry one line, while others are capable of carrying multi lines. Lines are attached to the planers and run at different depths. When a fish strikes, a release clip allows the line to break free from the planer, and the angler can engage the fish.

The Chesapeake Bay planer at work.

Enter Chesapeake Bay charter captains. Figuring bigger is better, they use a side planer with three planing surfaces that may carry four or five lines and be three or four feet across. Instead of the lines being connected directly to the planer, they are connected to the line running from the boat to the planer. A rubber band attached to a shower curtain clip is often used as a release clip. So now you have a boat that would normally pull 12 lines pulling another 10. Depending on the length of the line to the planer, the effective beam of the boat can grow by 20 to 30 feet.

To the best of my knowledge, these huge planers are not available from any major manufacturer. They are produced by the people who use them, and a few local builders in the Chesapeake Bay region. The various designs show considerable inspiration.

I do not recommend using these large side planers with trailer boats, but, of course, some anglers do. If you are very careful and realize that most people don't expect trailer boats to have lines sticking out 10 feet or more on either side of their normal width, you can effectively pull a side planer with an 8-foot beam boat. I have observed, however, on the crowded fishing grounds the captains of small boats with big planers shouting, pointing, and desperately trying to keep everyone from running over their lines.

A sister to the side planer is the dummy line. This is a heavy handline with a big weight trolled from the side of the boat. It is called a dummy line because it takes a dummy to pull it in. The weight is heavy enough to get the lure down below those trolled from rods and literally bounce on the bottom. A rubber strap is used to take up the shock of a strike. To some anglers who prefer fighting a fish with rod and reel, this approach verges on the questionable.

A more reasonable way to go deep is the downrigger. This is a device using a heavy wire line on a large spool that may be operated by hand or by an electric motor. The line plays out through a big swinging eye on the end of a short but sturdy rod. The other end of the wire line is attached to a very heavy, usually 12-pound, lead ball. Above the ball there will be at least one release clip where the running line from the fishing reel is attached. Up to three release clips may be used if the captain is very careful about his choice of lures and placement of the rods. The bottom line may take a shallow diving plug, but the other two need straight running lures to keep out of one another's way. In my experience, sticking with one lure per downrigger is easier and more productive.

To set the downrigger, first let the chosen lure out at least 50 feet behind the boat. Next attach the line to the release clip and lower the ball, using the drag on the downrigger wheel to slow the descent. The fishing reel must be in free spool, and the angler must control the line to prevent a backlash.

All downriggers have some type of counter to let the operator know how much line is out between the downrigger rod tip and the ball. This is not an accurate count of how deep the lure is running. While almost any lure will work in this configuration, including umbrellas and bucktails, a diving plug will run deeper than the ball, and some anglers feel this is an advantage. By working the diving plug below the ball, the fish at the same level as the lure are in no danger of being clunked on the head by 12 pounds of lead, or, at the very least, scared out of their wits when the ball comes past. Keep in mind that diving plugs put considerable strain on the running line and require a very snug setting of the release clip.

Also, the water pressure on the wire line will raise the ball higher in the water column than the counter indicates. Because the trolling speed for stripers is always as slow as the boat will go, this is not as big a difference as it would be at higher trolling speeds.

Downriggers may be permanently mounted on the boat, or they can be used with a base that sits in a rod holder. Choose a downrigger model with a holder for the downrigger rod. In the Great Lakes, anglers employ a very soft rod that is constantly bent double when in use. I tried one in salt water and found it also bent double when fighting a big fish. Now I use a regular trolling rod in the 20-pound class with good results.

Storage of the 12-pound lead ball and one or two replacements can be a challenge on a small boat. I have kept them in the ever-useful five-gallon bucket stowed in the cabin where it cannot fall on anyone. When in use it is a good idea to keep the ball in the water while resetting the line. A 12-pound ball can cause a lot of damage if left to swing around on the end of a wire line.

Another trolling aid is the diving planer. You can set it from a rod or on a handline. The diving planer will go deep without added weight, and if rigged on a handline with a release clip, the running line will pull free; the angler only has to crank in the fish.

Diving planers come in various sizes from one to four, with the largest saved for dredging out the deepest holes in the ocean or bay. These big boys are usually used on handlines because of the strain they would put on a rod and reel. I have used a number 3 diving planer on a handline, and just pulling it in was a workout. In theory, a planer is supposed to trip when slack is put in the line, but in real life this might or might not occur. I have had fair luck tripping a planer on a rod and reel when it was time to pull it up, but not much success when attempting the same thing on a handline. One trick you may want to try is using three or four feet of 200-pound leader attached to the planer with offshore crimps and chaff protectors. Attach the running or handline to the leader and hope for the best.

The normal setup is a number 1 or number 2 diving planer on a 30- or 50-pound outfit with a star drag. Lever drags tend to slip when under pressure from a diving planer. A 40- to 50-foot leader is not uncommon behind a planer, especially when you use a spoon. The leader is attached to the planer with a ball-bearing snap swivel and another swivel is often used halfway down the leader.

When setting a diving planer, first let out the lure and leader to be sure it is running free without any tangles. Next, put the planer in the water and give it a bit of slack until it sets. At this point the water pressure on the planer will pull it under and line must be let off the reel under thumb pressure to prevent a backlash. It is not necessary to let out a lot of line when fishing with a diving planer. I usually count to six (1-1,000, 2-1,000, etc.) when fishing in 20 to 40 feet of water and to ten in deeper water, or until I feel the planer hit bottom.

Diving planers may be used with mono, braid, and wire. Care must be taken with all three line types to prevent the line from burying under itself on the reel. If you choose braid, keep in mind that it will cut like a knife when under this much strain. Diving planers will also work on downriggers instead of the large lead ball. Planers, like downriggers, should be avoided in areas with rocky bottoms or other rig-grabbing obstructions. Losing this kind of hardware is an expensive proposition.

The author prefers bait casting but spinning gear will also produce when jigging.

Jigging

You should jig when stripers are in fairly deep water, from 20 to 100 feet, and holding tight to the bottom. The lure must be heavy enough to get down to the fish no matter how deep the water or how strong the current.

Jigging is usually done over some type of structure, be it rocks, a rip, or a wreck. It can also be productive when the stripers are holding on the downcurrent side of a bridge piling, where lighter lures will be washed away from the structure by the current.

These jigs will get down in fast running water.

I like a sturdy rod and conventional reel for jigging because I want the lure to react at the slightest twitch of the rod tip, and I can control the descent of the lure better with a conventional reel. For jigs up to three ounces in water between 20 and 50 feet deep, I use a TSCC 76IH Tsunami rod and an Ambassadeur 3004 Torno reel spooled with 30-pound Stren braid. In deeper water with jigs to six ounces, I use the SaltStik SSGT76H Fenwick rod, the 7000C Ambassadeur reel, and 50-pound Spiderwire line. I tie a 10- to 12-foot leader of 30- or 50-pound Fluorocarbon to the braid with an Albright knot.

Use a snap to connect a jig to the leader.

Attaching the jig to the leader can be done in several ways. If the jig has a split ring, just tie the ring directly to the leader. Jigs without a split ring should be attached by a black snap that has been tied to the leader. You can use a snap on a lure with a split ring, but it only adds extra hardware that serves no useful purpose other than allowing a quicker change of lures.

Attaching bucktails, plastic shads, and lead heads with plastic tails is normally done by tying the leader directly to the jig. I use the improved clinch knot because I like a direct connection that allows the lure to move at the slightest twitch of the rod tip. But many of my fishing companions use the loop knot because they like the jig to have more freedom to move around. We all catch stripers at the same rate.

When jigging, let the line fall directly alongside the boat or cast it out into the current so it will fall to the bottom as the current carries it to the boat. Control the descent with thumb pressure on the spool of the reel and be prepared for a strike at any point during the drop. When you feel the bottom, stop the descent and begin jigging the lure by raising the rod tip up and down. Be prepared to set the hook at any time, but especially on the drop, when many hits occur.

At some point you will no longer feel bottom and it will be necessary to allow more line to come off the reel until bottom contact is reestablished. At this point repeat the cycle until the water pressure against the line keeps the jig from reaching bottom. Now reel in and begin the process all over again.

Most anglers jig from drifting and anchored boats. I feel drifting is the most productive because you can cover more area and keep up with the fish when they are on the move. Rips are an ideal example of when drifting is very productive. By drifting over and through a rip, the lure will work from one side to the other and be seen by stripers holding

A conventional reel allows the angler to keep in constant contact with the jig.

from the top to the bottom. Unfortunately, I have seen anglers anchor over a good rip and thus make drifting very difficult for all the other boats in the area. True, the anchored boat can work a small area that is holding fish, but the captain is hogging it for himself, while a fleet of drifting boats could work the same area and everyone would have a shot at the fish.

While we have not yet discussed bait fishing, there is a good chance to catch stripers in a chunk slick on a jig. The chunks will bring stripers close to the boat, and while most will be taken on bait, jigs worked directly from the stern will pick up their share.

Jigging over a rip . . . pays off.

Another time when jigs may be productive is when stripers are attracting birds. Quite often boat traffic will put the birds and the fish down, but if you are marking fish on the bottom after the fleet blasts off following the birds, try dropping a jig down and working it at a slow pace. I have used the Hyper Striper jig in this situation with good results. In fact, the fish left behind are usually larger than those working right under the birds.

Jigs come in all shapes and sizes. For most applications I like a metal jig, such as those made by Stingsilver, Crippled Herring. Point

Judith, Yo-Zuri, Tsunami, Atom, and others. Bucktail-style jigs will also work, but they do not sink as fast as a metal jig. A lead head with a plastic tail does sink well and will have more action with less effort than a metal lure.

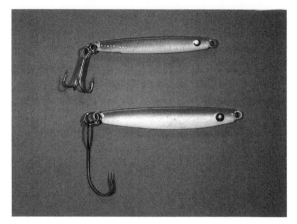

These metal lures will work when the local bait is long and slender.

Selecting the right jig for the occasion at hand requires a bit of observation. If the current is strong and the water deep, use a metal jig. In shallow water with not much current, a bucktail or plastic tail will do just fine.

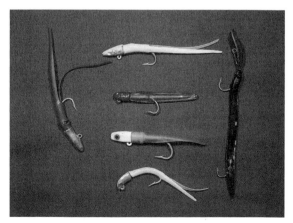

Bait tail jigs work well at night around a permanent light source.

Another factor in jig selection is the size and type of bait in the area. On a recent trip I observed the stripers were feeding on bait with a green back and silver underside. Fortunately, I had a metal jig with those identical markings and was able to catch more than my share of stripers.

In this case the bait was small herring or shad and the jig I chose was of this same shape. If the bait had been sand eels, I would have gone with a slender lure like one from Bridgeport, and if bunker were in the area, the Point Judith imitation would have been the choice.

Plastic shads are also good for jigging and work well with the up and down movement of the rod tip. The key is to be sure you have a shad heavy enough to reach bottom. On the trip mentioned above, several of my fellow anglers had a plastic shad with the same markings as the bait, but were unable to work the lighter lures down deep enough to find the fish.

Out in the deep water of the ocean or bay, jigs can be very effective. If you mark stripers on the bottom in 50 to 100 feet of water and try to troll past their position, the lure will only be in the strike zone for a few moments. Find those same fish and drift over them using a jig and you will have the lure in the strike zone for a much longer period of time. It is possible to keep catching stripers for quite some time if the drift imitates the movement of the stripers. Meanwhile, trollers will pick up one or two fish per pass, then have to turn around to make another run. Jigging allows the angler to feel the strike, while trolling leaves the hook-setting up to the boat. If you are trolling and keep getting hits in the same general area, you might want to stop over the fish and break out the jigs, if you will not be in the way of the other boats.

Five

Bait Fishing

So far we have addressed fishing with artificials, but now we will look at the way that bait catches many stripers. Striper bait can be anything from a live eel to a two-day old bunker head. It can be as large as a whole mackerel or as small as a grass shrimp. Stripers will eat just about anything they can catch, which helps them survive in a changing environment. During the spring they may eat white perch in the headwaters of the Chesapeake Bay and before the year is up they may be dining on bunker off the Cape Cod coast.

One note: Fishing with live large bait, such as live-lining bunker or spot, during periods of warm water, in the high 60- to 70-degree mark, can over-stress stripers, and the mortality rate can go up significantly. In warmer conditions, the angler has to make an ethical decision about artificials versus bait; if you're keeping your limit, using bait is legit, but for catch-and-release angling, lures are the way to go when the weather and water are warm.

Worms

One bait available throughout the striper's range is the sea worm. They are found everywhere in salt to brackish water and in some areas the hatch of a certain species will draw stripers from far and near.

Anglers from North Carolina to Maine use bloodworms, although this worm is harvested in the New England and Canada regions. Because the folks who pick and sell bloodworms

Worms, real or artificial, will catch stripers.

have a lock on the market, the price has risen to more than $10 a dozen in many areas. In recent years, products such as Fishbites and Gulp! have been replacing bloodworms in many applications, which may reduce the price of bloodworms as demand falls.

Blood and sandworms will take stripers throughout the season, but they seem to do their best work in the spring. Anglers use whole worms and worm pieces, but most striper fishermen use the entire worm. Surf fishermen rig bloodworms by putting the hook through the worm several times, making it almost into a ball, and then rig a second worm by putting the hook only in the head and allowing the body to stream out in the current.

A favorite shallow water trick is streaming a blood or sandworm behind a spinner blade and trolling slowly close to shore. Rowboats and kayaks are particularly adept at this technique.

In New England, anglers use a sandworm trailing behind a tube lure and fished on wire line to work the depths around rocks and ledges. The bait must be worked close to the rocks, and fishing such areas as Sow Reef and Pigs Reef can be very dangerous.

To rig the worm and tube, use a 10- to 20-foot leader running from the weight on the end of the wire to the tube. The length of the tube will be 12 to 36 inches, and the sandworm should be as long as possible. Hook the worm through the head and allow it to stream behind the tube, getting action as the tube spins.

Jim Travis, a New England guide, has good luck replacing the live sandworm with an imitation made by Exclude. These are scented artificial baits and seem to fool the bass just as well as the natural bait.

A lead head with a worm trailer worked very slowly across the bottom is a deadly technique almost anywhere stripers feed. It will work from the surf as well as from a boat, in both shallow and deep water. This setup can be very effective when fished from a jetty or along a rocky shoreline.

Keeping worms alive is not difficult. They like to be cool and damp, but not wet. Never let them touch fresh water. They are usually sold along with some seaweed that should be kept with the worms. A dozen worms will keep in the refrigerator for a week or so. Once they die, throw them out. I have tried freezing and salting bloodworms, and, while they are usable after such treatment, they are not particularly productive. This is another reason artificial worms are becoming so popular, because they will keep for a very long time and be just as good as when they were purchased.

Bunker

Another bait found throughout the striper's range is the bunker (or menhaden, or pogy). Anglers often rig a bunker live, but this bait is also deadly when cut up and fished behind a chunk slick. Increasingly, the bait of choice for

Bunker cut into chunks.

surf and boat fishermen is a bunker head fished on the bottom.

A live bunker is like candy to a striper. They target these oily baitfish because they somehow know bunker have higher nutrients than any other food source.

The problem faced by the striper fishermen is catching and keeping the bait alive. A cast net is good when bunker are near the surface, but a gill net will get them no matter where they swim. Local laws will dictate who may have and use gill or cast nets, and many places require a license to use any type of commercial gear. Check your local regulations before attempting any netting.

Gathering bunker bait from a pound netter.

Securing your own bunker will take time, and, on occasion, you may come up empty. For these reasons I prefer to buy my bait at the local tackle shop. Keeping a lot of bunker alive isn't easy, however, and many shops simply do not have the facilities. If this is the case in your area, catching the bait will be your only option. Because catching and keeping bunker alive is such a difficult undertaking for a tackle shop, do not expect bargains and get there early, before the other striper fishermen buy out the day's supply.

Once you have secured a supply of bunker, you must keep them alive. This requires a circular live well with a big pump to keep the water flowing. If bunker are placed in a square container, like a cooler, they will all swim to one corner and die. If the water flow is not strong, there will not be enough oxygen to keep the bunker alive. Most new boats come equipped with a suitable live well correctly placed and secured.

It takes a big circular live well with lots of running water to keep bunker alive.

If, like me, you have an older boat, there are several companies making tanks, pumps, and the necessary tubes and hardware to help you keep live bunker, or you can build your own live well out of a plastic barrel, a pump, and some tubes or pipes from the local Home Depot. Make sure you install the feed to the pump where it can pick up water while the boat is moving or at rest. The overflow pipe should never discharge on the deck, even if the boat is self-bailing. That much water has a way of getting into the bilge, so keep the outflow pipe flowing overboard and you won't have any surprises.

Keep in mind when locating the tank on board that water weighs about 6 pounds per gallon; 50 gallons equals 300 pounds. Water also has a bad habit of sloshing around, so it is like a 300-pound go-go dancer working out in the back of the boat.

To rig up for live bunker fishing I use a 5/0 to 7/0 circle hook on six feet of 50-pound fluorocarbon leader. There will be times when the stripers become line shy and you may need a leader as light as 20-pound test to draw strikes. My bunker rod is the Fenwick SaltStik SSGT76H with an Ambassadeur 7000HS reel filed with 50-pound braid. Spinning reels will also work and can be advantageous when you have to cast the bait to rocks or other structure that the boat cannot reach.

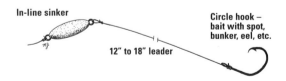

The standard live bait rig.

I have seen live bunker hooked in the tail, behind the dorsal fin, in the nose, and up through the chin and out of the nose. I prefer hooking mine either through the nose or up through the chin. A bunker does not swim

Hook a live bunker through the nose to keep him alive and frisky.

sideways or backwards so it seems to me that hooking one through the back or tail would not make a natural presentation. Stripers will swallow a bunker headfirst, so having the hook in the front of the fish will ensure that it makes it inside the striper's mouth.

Bunker will swim to the bottom looking for safety, and if a pack of stripers is down there, the bunker quickly reverse their course. At this point the bunker will appear very nervous on the surface, and this is usually followed by a loud splash as a striper strikes its prey. Often this first strike will only stun the bunker, and the striper will return to eat it in a matter of seconds. Never try to set the hook until you are sure the striper has the bait. This will be indicated by the line moving away at a faster speed than the bunker could swim.

To set a circle hook, point the rod tip towards the water and crank out the slack. When the line comes tight, the fish will be hooked. Circle hooks work so much better than J hooks, and the fish is almost always hooked in the corner of the mouth, so a release is much easier and safer for the fish.

As a general rule, the captain will go to a place where stripers are known to hang out, try to find them on his sonar, and then put the baits down. Most of the time the bunker will be fished without any weight, but in-line sinkers can be used if the bait needs encouragement to swim down to the stripers.

One place live bunker are used is the end of a jetty, or around big rocks close to the beach. Stripers like this structure and will stay close in, making trolling or drifting all but impossible.

In most cases, the captain will place the boat as close to the end of the jetty as he can without endangering the crew, while the angler casts the bunker to the structure. At this point, let the bait swim around on its own or work it very slowly back to the boat. Not every jetty and every rock will hold a striper, so this is a modified run-and-gun operation as the captain looks for action.

Bunker may become worn out when repeatedly cast and retrieved. A tired bunker does not act right and won't be able to make it to the bottom. At this point, the tired bunker should be replaced with a livelier neighbor. Do not throw the used bunker away. You never know how the day or night will play out, and a tired bunker is better than no bunker at all. If a bunker dies in the tank, get it out as soon as possible and put it on ice. A dead bunker is better than no bunker at all. You can distinguish a used bunker from a fresh one because the used fish will have a red nose.

Live bunker are occasionally used from the beach and jetty, but keeping them alive is a major task. If you can rig a circular live well on your surf fishing vehicle and keep it somehow supplied with running water, then bunker may be hauled around. To date, the only way I have seen live bunker used from a jetty or beach is

by catching them on site, either with a cast net or snag hook, and putting them back out.

I have tried hooking a bunker with a snatch hook and then letting it settle back down to the bottom. But I miss more fish than I catch using this method and have better success bringing the bunker back in and rehooking it with a circle hook.

Chunking

Cut, fresh bunker, while not as productive as the live version, will catch plenty of stripers, and many anglers are successful with this approach. You cut the bunker into chunks and toss these sparingly over the stern of a boat that is anchored in a likely location.

Captain John's E-Z Chunk saves time and fingers.

Cutting bunker into chunks is not the most enjoyable part of the trip, and Captain John Nedelka, of the *Karen Sue* out of Indian River, Delaware, has invented and patented a device that makes the job easier and faster. Captain John's E-Z Chunk will quickly chop the bunker with little chance of the operator cutting himself instead of the bait. A five-gallon bucker is placed below the E-Z Chunk machine. The bunker are placed on a grid of sharp blades while a handle lowers a set of op-

A bunker ready for chunking.

Or through the back right behind the head.

posing sharp blades on the fish. The result is nice, clean bunker chunks in the bucket.

The likely location for chunking could be a slough, a creek mouth, a bar, or any other bottom structure that may hold stripers. The captain will anchor so the chunks will be carried down current into the deeper part of the structure.

Once the chunks begin to draw stripers, most anglers will start by using a bunker head and a circle hook. I prefer to put the hook up through the chin and out the nose.

Hook a bunker chunk through the back.

A bunker tail may be hooked through the end or . . .

A bunker head may be hooked through the nose.

Others will hook the bait through the eyes or the top of the head. I do not use a fish-finder rig, but tie the 5/0 to 7/0 circle hook directly to a six-foot section of 80-pound mono leader. Tie the leader to a three-way swivel,

. . . through the back.

and tie a sinker capable of taking the bait to the bottom to one of the other eyes. I use 30-pound tackle for chunking because the size of the fish taken by this technique can be quite large.

You can also catch stripers in a chunk slick by hooking a chunk of bunker with the same size circle hook and drifting it back in the slick. I usually toss the chunk with the hook along with a handful of unhooked chunks to make a more natural presentation. Pull line off the reel as the bait sinks so there is always a loop of slack line on the surface of the water. Watch the fall rate of the hooked bait and make sure it stays with the unhooked chunks. The drag from the line can slow the descent, and if this happens put a small split shot or rubber core sinker on the line to bring everything together.

A general setup on a chunking boat includes two or three rigs set on the bottom with the rods in holders while the anglers on board each work a drifting bait. Keep in mind that you don't have to set a circle hook. Let the rods in the holders stay there until they bend over and line begins to come off the reel against the drag. Anglers fishing with drift baits should crank out all the slack after a pickup, and when the line comes tight the striper will be hooked.

If you can fish somewhere outside the fleet, the chances of drawing stripers to your boat will be increased. Unfortunately, any location that has a history of drawing big stripers will also draw a crowd. In this case, get there early and be the first with chunks in the water. The first chunk line the stripers find will hold their attention at least until you have your limit.

Successful chunking is dependent on the current. The chunks will distribute much better on a running current, making that the optimum time to be there. Once the tide changes, the strength of the current will diminish until slack water. Then it picks up again as it changes direction. At some point between the tide change and slack water, the current may be moving one way on top and the opposite way on the bottom. This will cause the chunks to go around in a circle and may slow the striper bite. Basically, there will be three to four hours of good current on any tide cycle, and the prudent angler will be there when the conditions are optimum.

When the current changes direction, you will probably have to move the boat. This requires pulling the anchor and repositioning the boat so the chunks once again are carried to the deeper part of the structure. Some structure will only be good on one direction of the current. In this case you will have to move the boat to another location where there is a better chance of attracting a bite.

Boat position should be planned before the trip. Use the latest navigation chart and tide table to plot likely spots, considering the direction of the current at the time of the trip. As an example, a slough that runs north to south with the tip at the north end will produce when the current is running to the south. The boat should be anchored at the tip so the chunks will be carried to the deeper part of the slough.

Once the direction of the current changes, the tip may not be so hot, but the edge of the slough may produce. If this does not work, look for a location where the south to north current will run from shallow water to deep. A good captain will plot out several possible locations on both stages of the current and put the coordinates in his GPS.

Chunking may also be done near bridges that hold stripers. The fish tend to lie under the bridge, and the stream of chunks may encourage them to venture out and find your hooked bait. In this situation, somewhat heavier tackle and a firm drag setting are required to convince the striper to stay in open water and not go back under the bridge.

When the current is running hard, put a swimming plug 50 to 75 feet behind the boat and let it move with the current. Place the rod in a holder and forget about it until the clicker begins to scream. It is also possible to fool a striper with a bucktail or other jig bounced along the bottom in a chunk slick. This should only be done when it does not interfere with the normal chunking operation.

Chunking may attract the attention of some less than desirable species. Bluefish can move in and eat everything in sight. If the blues take over from the stripers, you can always break out the light tackle, a few metal lures or poppers, and have some fun. If that does not suit your plans, it will be necessary to pull the anchor and go off in search of stripers at another location.

The ever-popular spiny dog shark has increased in population and range along the northeast coast. Once these slim fish find your chunk slick, the only solution is to pack up and leave.

Surf

Cut bunker has become the number-one go-to striper bait for surf fishermen and is accounting for some very big bass along the beach. With the minimum size in the ocean currently at 28 inches, it does not pay to fish for little stripers, so rig up a big bait on heavy tackle.

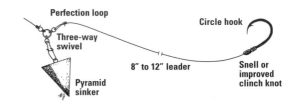

A bait fishing bottom rig for the surf.

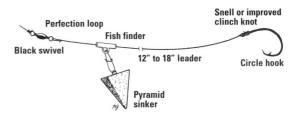

The fish-finder rig is normally used with live bait.

I use a whole bunker head on a 7/0 circle hook tied to six to eight inches of 80-pound test fluorocarbon leader. The leader is secured to a three-way swivel with an improved clinch knot. The sinker is attached to the swivel with a large snap. Some surf casters prefer to use a fish-finder rig, but I believe the three-way swivel rig is more efficient, especially with the circle hook. All I have to do when a fish hits is crank out the slack and the striper will hook himself.

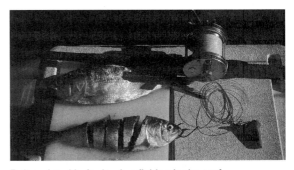

Bait and tackle for bunker fishing in the surf.

The fish-finder is also more difficult to cast, because the sinker can slide down the line. There are several modified versions of the fish-finder rig that use a short leader between the sinker and the bait, but I still prefer the three-way swivel rig.

Hook the bunker head through the nose for better casting distance.

Casting distance is always important in the surf, but many times stripers will be right in or just beyond the wash. I try to place my cast on the far side of the breaking waves and work it slowly to the beach. I am currently using an Ambassadeur 9000 reel filled with 50-pound Stren braid on a Tsunami TSTSC 1102XH rod. I attach a 50-pound mono shock leader to the braid with an Albright knot. A spinning outfit that will fill the bill would be something like a Jarvis Walker 8500 on a Tsunami TSTSS 1102XH rod. Fill the reel with the same 50-pound Stren braid and 50-pound mono shocker.

There will be times when the stripers may be feeding farther off the beach and a longer cast will be required. Distance casting requires practice, and if you do not live near the water, try to find a football field or similar area and keep trying until you can put an eight-ounce sinker out 450 feet or more. The pendulum cast, brought to this country by English long distance caster John Holden, can be modified to work with an eight-ounce sinker and a bunker head. The idea is to load the rod as much as possible before launching the rig. As a right-hander, I begin my cast by turning my upper body to point the rod behind my back, the tip at slight diagonal to the ground and pointing at two o'clock (lefties do this to their left side). I swing the rig along my right side with a smooth motion until it is in position to cast and then let it go. Smooth is the operative word here; a jerky swing will not put the proper load on the rod.

I know we should never put a surf rod in a sand spike while fishing because we should keep in constant contact with our baited hook, but everyone does. Here too the circle hook helps catch the striper while we are sitting in a beach chair or on the back of our buggy. When you put the rod in a sand spike, be sure the drag is properly adjusted on the reel, or you may watch as your entire rig disappears into the waves. Don't ask how I know, but if your reel goes under water in the surf, it will never work properly again, because all of that fine sand carried in the wash will infiltrate the inner workings of the reel.

When you run out of bunker heads, try the tail section. I cut it off about three to four inches from the end and hook the bait at the point where the tail fin meets the body. The tail is more likely to spin than the head and hooking it like this does diminish the problem.

The body of the bunker does not have much holding ability on the hook. If you are going to use chunks of the body, hook them through the back at the thickest part of the chunk. I would check the bait every 10 to 15 minutes, no matter what part I am using.

Eels

Using eels as striper bait should probably be illegal. The slimy things will catch stripers everywhere on both day and night tides with an efficiency that is almost unsporting.

Eels are so deadly on stripers they should be outlawed. (Keith Kaufman photo.)

While you can pot your own eels, there might be laws in your area that require a commercial license to operate an eel pot. I always purchase my eels from a local tackle shop, and during the height of the season they can run $1.50 each or more. If you have your boat in a slip or have access to the water, eels can be stored in a live cart for future use. Almost any type of cart will work so long as the holes are small enough to keep the eels inside. Some carts are built with a wood frame and screen. Others are made from a plastic five-gallon bucket with small holes drilled around the sides.

To carry the eels from the cart or tackle shop, one of those small Igloo lunch coolers is ideal. Put in some ice and a little bit of water, then dump in the eels. The ice will slow them down and it will be easier to put one on a hook. A mesh bag will keep the eels in one place, rather than squirming all over the cooler.

Keep eels in a bucket or cooler with some ice to slow them down.

When it is time to fish, grab the eel with a rag and put the hook up through both lips. Some anglers will put the hook in the mouth and out one eye, but I think the first method keeps them alive a little longer and makes a more natural presentation.

Drifting Eels

When drifting eels along the bottom, I use a three-way swivel rig. I tie or snell a 5/0 to 7/0 circle hook to six feet of 50-pound fluorocarbon leader, then to one eye of the three-way swivel. A sinker heavy enough to carry the rig to the bottom is tied to the other eye using two to three feet of 30-pound line. I use two double surgeon loops on this line, one large enough for the sinker and the other looped through the eye of the swivel. The eel will be hooked up through the bottom jaw and out the top of the mouth.

In every aspect of live eel fishing, it is absolutely critical to keep the eel stretched out so it cannot twist itself and the leader into a hopeless mess. To this end, drop the eel overboard as soon as you have it hooked and let it sink to the bottom as you control the descent.

Hooking an eel through the mouth makes for a more natural appearance.

High Level Bridge at the mouth of Chesapeake Bay, to the shoals outside of Oregon Inlet.

There is, as of this writing, a possibility that eels will become illegal to use as bait. The NOAA Fisheries and the Atlantic States Marine Fisheries Commission are putting together an eel management plan that could place a moratorium on eels until they recover from what some think is a depleted state. At this point, the summer of 2006, I have no idea what the plan will call for or when, if ever, it will go into effect.

Casting

When stripers are holding in a location where drifting is impossible, casting live eels comes into play. This is bit more difficult than drifting because the eel must be kept on the move by the angler, without much help from the current.

If you let it down too fast, the eel will have a chance to meet the running line and the two will have a quick marriage. This is not a good thing. Let the rig down at such a speed as to keep the eel stretched out in the current, away from the running line and the leader.

Once the eel is safely down, it may be necessary to let out line in order to keep the sinker on the bottom. Do this very carefully, because any slack given to the eel will encourage it to do mischief.

When the current is not too strong and the water less than 50 feet deep, you might be able to put the rod in a holder and drift along until a striper takes the eel. I know quite a few charter captains who do this for inexperienced patrons who might miss a strike if allowed to hold the rod. The circle hook does the skill work, and all the party has to do is reel in the striper. This technique also works for the most experienced anglers.

Drifting with live eels is done everywhere from New England to North Carolina with great success. As with all types of striper fishing, structure is the most important thing, and it varies from rocks and rips up north, to the

Casting with an eel can be productive on day or night tides.

The rig changes a bit from drifting to casting. The three-way swivel is gone and the leader is attached to the running line with a black snap swivel. If you must add a sinker, place it between the running line and the leader. Put the hook up through the bottom jaw and out the top of the mouth of the eel.

When an eel is cast to structure, you should retrieve it slowly, but with enough pressure on the line to keep the eel running straight. You want it to look like it is swimming free without actually letting it do so.

Jetties are a favorite location for casting eels from a boat. Toss the bait as close as possible to the structure and bring it slowly back to the boat. With a bit of experience you will be able to let the eel swim down into the rocks for a moment before pulling it back out. This will attract the striper's attention, because he will see a tasty morsel getting away.

When casting, you'll need to let the striper have the eel for a second or two before letting the line come tight. No need to count to 100 or whatever we used to do before circle hooks. Just a one- or two-count is all that is required for the striper to turn with the eel and the circle hook to penetrate.

Once hooked, you'll need a bit of brute force to pull the striper to open water. As a rule, once the striper is out of the rocks it will not make any concerted effort to return, preferring to wage battle in open water. Notice that I said "as a rule"; there are always stripers who are more than willing to break the rules.

Other types of structure where casting eels is productive include bridge pilings, piers, rocks, and shallow water wrecks.

Surf

I have a friend in Long Island who claims that he never uses bait when striper fishing. When I asked him what he calls eels, he replies that they are "living lures." What he means is eels are fished in the surf the same way you would fish a plug, although this strikes a pretty tight definition between "living lure" and "live bait." My friend casts and retrieves eels like a lure and they are never allowed to sit on the bottom the way one might fish a bunker head. Should you allow a live eel to sit on the bottom, it would quickly tangle up the leader, rig, and running line into an ungodly mess.

A surf rig is a little different than a live eel drift rig, more like a casting rig. Because long casts are seldom necessary from a boat, a three-foot long leader is not a problem. On the surf, where long casts are the norm, a shorter leader, say, 12 to 18 inches, is more practical. In fact, you can tie the hook directly to the shock leader and eliminate the short leader to the eel. When the surf is calm, the eel can be fished without weight, but when the water is rough, a sinker is necessary and will be attached 18 to 36 inches above the eel. Use a torpedo or rubber core sinker for this application.

Cast the eel into the surf and retrieve it back to the beach with a slow but steady action. Keep it coming right into the wash, as stripers often lay in very close. Most of the time a fan cast pattern works best, and you can cover a lot of water without moving. Once you have worked one section of beach, move on to the next.

While hooking an eel in the head is the accepted practice, in the surf my friend Jim Hutchinson, Jr., from New Jersey, hooks an eel in the tail and fishes it with a fish-finder rig.

The idea is to let the eel run free, taking line off the reel as it seeks shelter in rocks or other structure. Jim claims so long as the eel feels pressure on its tail, it will swim away from the line and not tangle everything up.

If you are fishing the end of a bar or any place where the current moves past, try to place the eel into the current so it will sweep past your position. Keep the tip of the rod pointed towards the point where the line enters the water and retrieve the line to maintain contact with the eel. Almost all live eel surf fishing is done at night, and since it is really bad form to shine a light on the water, it will be necessary to develop a touch for this type of fishing. This cannot not be taught; it has to come from experience.

It is also important to note that the current flow will change throughout the tide cycle, and adjustments must be made to the retrieve in order to keep the eel in the strike zone. During times of maximum current flow you might have to add some weight, while a slower current may be fished without a sinker.

In most cases, a striper will take up station where the current flows past, but not directly in the current. The eel must swim along the bottom and wash past the striper's position in order to grab his attention. It may take several casts before you get the retrieve down and put the bait in the proper place. Once again this is a matter of experience. If you are fishing with other folks and they are catching and you are not, watch what they do very carefully, then do the same. In some locations a picket line will form, with anglers taking the point until they hook up. They then move down the line so the next angler can cast to the hot spot. Yes, you really need to be in the right place, and, yes, stripers are that focused on one area.

Current flow will also affect the open surf. The best technique is to begin by casting into the current and let the eel wash past your position as you keep tension on the line. Keep casting in the fan pattern, because every cast will work with the current and wind to put the eel in a slightly different place.

Speaking of wind, some of the best surf fishing occurs during times when the wind is strong onshore. Having a live eel blown back in your face is not something most people enjoy, so a weight will be needed to carry the bait to the stripers. Placing a sinker on the line does provide more weight, but also sends the rig tumbling and turning through the air, which does not help with casting efficiency. Fortunately, the onshore wind pushes bait and the stripers very close to the beach, so a long cast is seldom required.

Inlets

Inlets attract stripers that often chase bait inside or corner it at the entrance. Drifting a live eel through the inlet or casting it from the shoreline can be highly productive.

Most inlets have some sort of sandbar just inside at a point where the current begins to slow and deposits sand. Stripers will often hold here waiting for bait to pass by. When possible, drift your live eel along the edge of the bar, allowing it to move from shallow to deep. In most cases the water depth will be less than 30 feet, so the eel will move along just fine without additional weight.

In the deeper parts of the inlet, a weight will be needed due to the strength of the current. Stripers will hold behind some kind of bottom structure, so the eel must bounce along the bottom and over the structure.

From shore or from the jetty that protects the inlet, eels are cast and retrieved just like a lure. Often the stripers will be holding right in the rocks, or at any point where there is a break in the jetty. Eels placed in such structure do not have a long life expectancy.

For some reason, eels drifted through the inlet produce on day and night tides, while those cast to the jetty are much more productive at night. Inlets will produce on all tides, but you will need to find the hot spots for each stage. Rarely will you ever have one location at an inlet that works on every stage of the tide.

Dead Eels

You don't see many people fishing with a dead eel anymore, but it was once a very popular method. Today, the availability of live eels makes using dead ones almost unnecessary.

The easiest way to rig a dead eel is to put an eel jig, like the ones made by Point Judith lures, in the head of the deceased critter. Once so rigged, fish the dead eel just like a live one.

Back in the day, before there was stuff like GPS, my buddies and I would catch eels and put them in a salt brine that killed them almost instantly. After a few days in the salt we would take the eels out and rub them with a Brillo pad to remove the slime and give them a dark blue hue. Then began the fun part. We would use a rigging needle to thread a section of Dacron line from the eel's vent to his mouth. We tied a hook to the vent end of the line and pulled it inside the eel, with only the curve and the barb exposed. Then we tied the tag end of the line to the base of the hook on an eel jig, and the finished product fished pretty well. I

have not gone to that much trouble to rig a dead eel in over 20 years and do not have plans to do so anytime in the future. What we created back then has been replaced by big, soft plastics.

In some places, anglers cut eels into pieces and fish them on the bottom. The upper portion of Delaware Bay is one of the places where this is practiced, mostly by shore fishermen. They do catch a fair number of stripers and lots of big catfish on the eel chunks.

Sand Eels

As live bait, sand eels don't work too well, but they can be used dead as dressing on a jig or alone on a bottom rig. They are not the toughest bait, so some care must be used when hooking and casting. In my experience, when bass are on sand eels, a tube or thin metal lure is as good, if not better, than the real thing. Let the lure sink to the bottom and then work it with a quick jerk up before letting it sink to the bottom again. Try to imitate a sand eel coming up from the bottom. In the surf, stick baits are deadly, especially after dark.

Herring, Shad, Mackerel, Spot, and Other Baits

We know that stripers will eat anything that does not eat them first, so almost anything that swims in their range is fair game. Herring and shad are two favorites that usually attract attention during the spring run. Both of these fish behave like striped bass, spawning in the spring in the same general area as the stripers. Stripers do not exactly go on a hunger strike when on their spawning run, but the cold water and the business of reproducing do make them a little bit lethargic. Once the spawn is complete and the big cows move towards the open ocean, they encounter the shad and herring and the feed is on. Both of these baits work well alive, but like menhaden, they are difficult to keep that way.

A live herring can be used from the beach, jetty, or boat by hooking it through the nose and letting it swim. You can catch hickory shad with a net and use them like herring.

Years ago I caught herring on shad darts from the spillway at Records Pond in Laurel, Delaware. I did not try to keep them alive, but used them as cut bait in the surf. Others used cut herring in the Nanticoke River to catch some pretty big stripers.

In recent years, the herring run in Laurel has dwindled, but some anglers will still catch herring there and in other spillways and transport them to the inlet in tanks. I have been catching hickory shad out of Indian River Inlet and using them as cut fresh bait. If nothing else, the run to the beach is much shorter from the inlet than it is from Laurel.

There is a catch-and-release season on the Susquehanna Flats at the head of the Chesapeake Bay, and, while most local guides would much rather catch their stripers on jigs, plugs, and flies, when the water is cold and dirty, they will switch to cut herring. Some anglers become upset by this use of bait on spawning stripers, but when used with circle hooks I expect the mortality is about the same as with lures.

Live Atlantic mackerel, also known as Boston mackerel, is a favorite bait from New York north. They are generally jigged up on mackerel trees, then put right back over and used as a live bait. This is a late spring and into the summer fishery, when the mackerel are in spawning schools.

In the southern part of the striper's range, we use cut mackerel for fishing in the surf and occasionally from boats. When we have a spring mackerel run, the fish are almost always 10 to 12 miles offshore. We all know that fishing for stripers beyond the three-mile limit is illegal, so while dropping a live mackerel back down out there could catch a striper, it could also garner the angler a federal summons.

Spot also has become a top striper bait, especially from southern New Jersey to North Carolina. They can be caught with a cast net, a trap, or on hook and line. They are also carried in most tackle shops in areas where spot are popular as bait.

My angling buddies and I catch them by baiting a number-10 or number-12 hook with a very small piece of bloodworm and fishing around docks or other structure. Sometimes the spot will be in the shallow part of the inland bays around grass flats.

Spot will stay alive in almost any type of live well.

Once we have a few dozen in the live well, we head off to the striper grounds. Spot do very well in a live well without running water. I have a 30-gallon tank with an aerator that will keep up to three dozen spot happy all day. I do change the water once an hour by dipping out as much as I can and refilling the tank with fresh salt water.

Hook a spot through the eye sockets for best results.

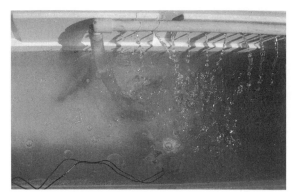

The cooler live well at work.

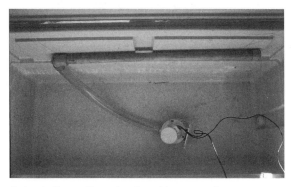

A simple live well can be rigged in any cooler.

Back when big weakfish roamed the surf in the fall, we would rig up a cooler with a bilge pump, some PVC pipe, and a hose to keep our spot alive on the beach. I have no doubt that live spot would work on the stripers in the surf, but by the time the stripers move into the beach the spot run is about over.

Indian River Inlet in Delaware and Ocean City Inlet in Maryland see a lot of big stripers caught on live spot. Anglers work the live spot close to the jetty as well as out in the inlet until they locate a concentration of stripers. Once this area has been identified, the entire fleet moves in, putting the stripers down, and the search must begin again. The boats at Indian River Inlet on a fall Saturday morning stretch from one side to the other and from the entrance of North Shore Marina to beyond the inlet bridge. Just about all of the anglers on these boats are drifting with live spot.

At the Chesapeake Bay Bridge Tunnel in Virginia, fishing live croaker as bait takes the stripers. The Virginia spring striper season is open until June 15 only, and this is the start of the croaker invasion, so the timing is perfect. The croaker are caught in the back bays or right along the bridge, and then dropped over the rocks that cover the two tunnels. The action is usually nonstop when the stripers are there, and most of them are good-sized.

Unethical "anglers" sometimes opt for the illegal method of using undersize weakfish in place of the croakers. The little trout are sometimes easier to find and catch than the croakers and unscrupulous people will take advantage of this situation. Apprehending these felons is next to impossible, so the practice will continue.

Scup

The scup, or porgy, is a natural bait for stripers that can be used live or dead. The most effective method is to catch the scup and then live-line them back down to the waiting bass.

Locating the bait may take some time, like all other fish, because scup will move their feeding location from one day to the next. Once you have a few dozen in the live well, the next step is finding some hungry stripers.

In New York and New England where scup are plentiful, most anglers use them over rips and around live bottom where mussels and other shellfish live. Scup have to meet a minimum legal size as bait in numerous places. So be sure to check local regulations before catching a live well full. Drifting is the most popular technique, but at times the scup may be live-lined to striper-holding locations in shallow water.

The tackle for fishing live scup is relatively heavy, especially when working fast, deep water. A circle hook in the 8/0 to 9/0 size is rigged on a three to four-foot length of 50-pound leader, and because the scup are large and may take the striper awhile to swallow, a fish-finder rig is employed. Keep in mind the scup must be of legal size and will weigh over a pound. Combine this with a sinker that could top 10 ounces and the need for heavy tackle is apparent. Also, a striper that can handle a bait of this size will probably be fairly large.

With a fish-finder rig, you'll need to allow the striper to take some line until he has the bait in his mouth. At that time, crank out all the slack, and when the line comes tight the circle hook will have done its job.

Snapper Blues

Bluefish make a hardy bait that will keep working long after a menhaden or herring has given up the ghost. Here, too, you will have to catch your own bait, and that in itself can be fun. Blues like moving water, much like menhaden,

so a circulating live well is the best choice for keeping them alive.

As with all other live baits, hooking the blue in the mouth or in the eye sockets will keep them alive and moving in a natural manner. Here, too, the local laws must be observed as to size limits. Where a snapper used as bait must be 10 to 12 inches or longer I still like a circle hook on a fish-finder rig for catching stripers.

Clams

Clams have been a favorite striper bait for many years. The crews on head and charter boats in the Chesapeake Bay would grind up soft shell clams to use as chum, then bait with the same to catch coolers full of pan rock. The demise of the soft shell and the rise of the bunker have changed chumming habits in this area.

I have seen some anglers using razor clams in the Chesapeake. These are long and thin, with a brittle shell.

In New Jersey, fishing with whole clams from the surf after a hard northeast blow is a well-used striper technique, as the storm will have pushed clams into the beach and broken them up in the wash. Anglers also chum with clams in Raritan Bay during the spring and early summer.

Today when we say "clams" we are talking about the big surf clams or quahogs. These are caught in the ocean, and most go to processing plants to be used in chowder or clam strips. Some find their way to tackle shops where they are sold to striper fishermen.

You don't have to be gentle when opening a surf clam. Slam two together and at least one will break open. Dig out the meat and toss the shells overboard to act as chum.

Clams have a tough foot and a very soft stomach. Use the foot as bait and the stomach as chum. Most of the time the foot will receive the hook and the stomach will go along for the ride. The soft part will last a little while in the water when fished from a boat, but often flies off when cast from the beach.

Some anglers will collect all the soft parts and put them in a mesh bag along with some shells for weight. The bag will be lowered to the bottom and act as chum to draw stripers to the bait.

Even the foot of a clam is not that tough and will come off the hook much sooner than a chunk of bunker or other fish. It also attracts all the little bait stealers in the vicinity, and they quickly gobble the clam without the angler feeling a thing. Because of this, keep checking a clam rig at least every 10 minutes.

Squid

Squid is the universal bait for all saltwater fish and will catch its share of stripers. Most anglers cut squid into strips and use them as a teaser behind a bucktail or jig. Squid can also be used on metal lures to put a scent trail in the water, as well as act as an attractor.

In parts of New England the striped bass is known as the "squid hound." Bob Pond invented the reverse Atom to imitate a squid, and there are stories of stripers chasing squid across the surface of the Cape Cod Canal. In this part of the world anglers commonly fish whole fresh squid from the beach as well as from boats.

In recent years bait shops have begun selling large squid that are cleaned, and these make great strip baits. The body is thick and very white so the strips stay on the hook through repeated casts. Another kind of squid

sold as bait comes from California and is much smaller. It could be used whole for stripers, but anglers usually cut it into strips, too.

Few anglers south of New England use squid as striper bait on a regular basis. However, a flounder or croaker fisherman can sometimes catch a decent striper on his squid strip.

Crabs

Stripers will eat both hard and soft crabs during times of the year when they are available. Because a striper does not have crushing teeth like a tog or red drum, they won't go after a full grown hard crab unless there is nothing else available. On the other hand, stripers will devour soft crabs or juveniles at any opportunity.

Hook a crab bait through one of the leg holes.

Spring is the best time to fish with peeler crabs, because this is when hard crabs molt. A peeler is a crab that is ready to molt and leave its hard shell. Once the crabs emerge from the shell, they are soft for several hours and become an easy target for every predator in the sea. While some anglers use a soft crab in the Chesapeake Bay, I personally would rather eat a soft shell than catch a striper.

To use a peeler (known as a "shedder" in New Jersey), the top shell is removed and the body cut into sections. You can get as many as six sections out of each body, depending on the size of the crab. The claws may be used by carefully cracking the shell and putting the hook through the joint. The apron is considered a prime piece of peeler crab bait.

Each section will have holes where the legs were attached. This is where the hook should be placed. If the hook is placed through the shell, the shell will crack and the bait will fall off the hook. Peeler crab does not stay on the hook very well to begin with, so every precaution must be made to make it as secure as possible.

While all crabs go through the molting process, most of the ones used for bait are blue crabs. There are different laws in each state as to the size and the seasons for blue crabs, so if you try to catch your own, be aware of the most current regulations.

Cut hard crabs will work on stripers, but are not a common bait. If you do use a hard crab, prepare it as you would a soft crab. I have used speckled or calico crabs that were stealing my bait in the surf by cutting them up and sending the pieces back out to see if anyone was interested in a crab dinner.

In certain parts of the Chesapeake Bay, anglers float live soft crabs back into grass beds where stripers are hunting. The crabs stay close to the surface, and when a striper finds one he can't believe his good fortune. The strike is loud and definite. This is a nighttime tactic.

You have to be careful when you hook a soft shell crab that you don't lose it, so set the line out with very little pressure. But you can secure the soft crab to the hook with a rubber band. In addition to stripers, this technique also produces weakfish, speckled trout, and red drum.

The more common use of a soft crab is to cut it into pieces and fish it on the bottom. Here you are likely to catch everything from bluefish to croaker.

Shrimp

The most popular way to fish for stripers with grass shrimp is to set anchor and chum. The back bays of New Jersey and Delaware lend themselves to this process. Anglers ladle the grass shrimp from an anchored boat, and sometimes sand is mixed with the shrimp to add to the dispersion. Anchoring below a creek mouth or other drain from a marsh is the best method.

Once the shrimp begin to draw stripers, the angler may float a few grass shrimp on a small circle hook back to the fish. Any number of lures might also be employed. This is a great opportunity for fly fishermen to ply their trade. Spin fishermen will use small bucktails, plastic shads, D.O.A. shrimp, shad darts, or Speck Rigs tipped with grass shrimp. If the action becomes really hot, a popper may produce some exciting strikes.

This technique is best in sheltered water well away from any channel or area where power boats are likely to pass by. An early outgoing current will put the angler on the water at the most opportune time of day. Be there before the sun is up and you should not be hampered by boat traffic or most other fishermen.

Sand Fleas

Sand fleas, also known as mole crabs, can be found by digging in the wet sand of a beach after a wave passes by. Small children love this sport, and the enterprising angler can acquire a good supply of bait by simply showing his or anyone else's children how much fun it is to dig up the little critters. Failing that approach, there are devices made for the purpose of digging fleas that allow the operator to stand while working. Local tackle shops will stock a supply of sand fleas—just be sure to get them live, not frozen. Frozen fleas will work on tog, but I have had little luck using them on stripers.

Sand fleas are effective on stripers in the surf and around rocks at inlets or jetties. I put two on one circle hook and fish them as close to the wash as possible. In the rocks, I drift them along with little or no weight.

Six

Surf Fishing

Surf fishing is the most challenging method to catch stripers and it just keeps getting more popular. I grew up reading stories by Frank Woolner and others about giant stripers along the coast caught on big plugs tossed into an angry surf by men using Penn Squiders with linen line on Calcutta rods. They roamed the beach in converted WWII jeeps or Model A Fords and were a force to be reckoned with. These were true pioneers who built their own rods, modified their reels, and carved their plugs out of wood. Bob Pond and Stan Gibbs were among these early striper fishermen, and both of their products are still on the market 60 years later.

Today we have carbon fiber rods, reels with magnetic breaks, and superstrong, ultrasensitive lines braided out of space-age materials. My Chevy Avalanche has the power to pull me through any type of sand, and the anodized aluminum rod rack on the front will carry a 100-quart cooler. Inside the truck I have heated leather seats, a CD player, and OnStar. I buy my plugs from a tackle shop and most of them are made from plastic. Modern surf fishermen have many advantages over their early counterparts, but the stripers are just as difficult to catch, even if we are more comfortable while pursuing them.

Reading the Beach

With stripers available all along the Atlantic coast from Maine to North Carolina and in the west along the California to Oregon shoreline, there will be any number of different beach structures that can hold fish. If you fish in one location only, finding the good spots

Rods rigged and ready for casting to surf stripers.

will be easier, and you should be able to go back to the same location on the same tide and expect somewhat similar results. The only time the beach structure will change is after a strong onshore wind accompanied by big seas. Even then, you won't take too long to relocate the good structure again.

The traveling surf caster must read the beach at every location where he fishes. He needs to find good structure as quickly as possible and be able to fish it correctly.

The best time to read a beach is at low tide when the bottom structure is exposed. You should find an observation post above the beach, either on a dune or boardwalk, with a

view of as much of the surf as possible. But don't ramble all over the dunes, especially if there are laws against it, because they suffer erosion easily.

The first place to look is the exposed beach. Try to find runouts where the water has carved channels in the sand or left a pond that will empty into the surf. Look at the structure of the beach. If it falls off gradually towards the water, it will probably be shallow for quite a ways out. When the beach drops off quickly, it indicates deep water close to shore.

Big or little points are going to hold fish sometime during the tide cycle. Some points, like the one on Hatteras Island, are immense, with dangerous waves and currents that attract stripers but make fishing for them an adventure. Smaller points are found on almost every beach and will also attract bait and stripers, on a much smaller scale.

Rocks cover much of the beach in New England and on the West Coast, posing an interesting situation for surf casters. The marine growth on the rocks draws in bait and the stripers will follow, but walking on these rocks is not for the ill equipped. In many cases there

Rocky beaches are common in New England and along the West Coast.

will be larger rocks just off shore that will be covered during some part of the high tide. Sensible anglers stand on shore and cast to these rocks. In some areas, like Long Island, there is a cadre of surf fishermen that swim out to these rocks and fish from there. A few don't even bother with the rocks, they just lay on their backs in wet suits and cast while propelling themselves along with swim fins. I am not sure if this qualifies as surf fishing—it's called "skishing"—but, if you've got the nerve and the life insurance is paid up, it's an option (not one I'm recommending).

Once you have an idea of the above-water structure, take a look at the waves to figure out what is beneath them.

The slough between the outer bar and the beach will often contain stripers.

Waves break when the water under them is one-and-a-half times their height. This means if a two-foot wave is breaking, the water there is three feet deep. If there is an area adjacent to the breaking waves that remains calm, the water there is deeper than three and a half feet. Chances are good that stripers will be in the deeper water. This deeper water may be a runout from the beach to even deeper water

offshore, or it may be a break in the bar. In either case, stripers will use the area to travel from in- to offshore or perhaps stage there waiting for food to pass by. In all cases, these are locations that deserve some consideration when seeking stripers.

In clear water you might be able to see holes off the beach, as they appear to be a deeper blue in color. When the water is turbid these holes are less easy to find, but may appear as slightly calmer in the center with riffles around the edges.

A really good fishing zone develops when an offshore bar comes into the beach. Often this appears as if the bar is coming in and the beach is moving out to meet it. The result is a deep hole close to the beach with a shallow sandbar that closes it off on one end. Stripers will push bait in here to trap it, and then feed at will.

Here the outer bar meets the beach creating a pocket that holds bait and attracts stripers.

A similar structure occurs where a jetty meets the sand beach. Bait moving along the beach will be pushed into the pocket and stripers will block their escape. One side of a jetty will always be deeper than the other due

The pocket where a jetty meets the beach will also trap bait.

The sight of birds working over fish in the surf will get a surf caster's blood boiling.

to the littoral drift. Sand will be scoured out of one side of a jetty and move along the beach until it encounters another jetty, where it will build up. As a general rule, the deeper side will be the most productive when fishing from the beach.

After observing the structure of a beach, you must figure out where and how to fish there. We have heard that stripers like structure in every type of fishing discussed so far, and surf fishing is no different. They will move along an open beach looking for a deep hole, runout, slough, or other structure where they can set up shop and ambush some bait. If, for example, they find a deep hole along a sand beach, they may sit on the bottom and wait for the bait to swim overhead. At the end of a runout, they will hold station waiting for the current to carry bait out from the beach. On a point, they will stage along the end of the downcurrent side and grab the bait as it washes past. An outer bar may be patrolled by stripers looking to feed on bait holding tight to the bar, with their concentration on the turbulence overhead.

Then there is the blitz. This is the absolute epitome of striper fishing, as the fish bust through the waves chasing bait and just about any lure you can place in their path. With screaming gulls overhead, the wind blowing hard onshore, and stripers on every cast, this is as close to heaven as it gets. I have experienced this just once with striped bass while on a vacation to Cape Cod, and it is something I will never forget and hope someday to repeat.

Different beach structure will fish differently on each stage of the tide. A deep hole will be good on the ebb when bait has nowhere else to go. A runout is best on a falling tide, as the bait is washed to the waiting stripers. The slough between the outer bar and the beach is best on the flood, when stripers will come over the bar looking for food. Rocks work best when they are at least partially covered with water and the stripers can hide behind them waiting for a meal. Along every beach there is somewhere to fish on every stage of the tide. The angler's job is to read the beach and figure out where and when those locations will produce.

Jetties

Jetty fishermen are a breed apart. They climb out on slippery rocks during the darkest night, and, while any sane person would like some

Jetty fishermen perch on rocks much like birds.

Jetty fishermen need the proper footwear.

company on such an adventure, they are more than happy when left alone.

The one piece of gear that a jetty jockey must have is a set of creepers—the metal-spiked sandals that an angler can attach to his wader boots. I use Korkers, but have employed golf shoes, rubbers with spikes in the bottom, and

a custom pair made from stainless steel. To go out on a jetty without creepers is to ask for, at the least, some broken bones.

Every jetty is different, but all are alike. They all extend into the water, and the material used to construct them attracts all forms of sea life. Jetties also offer the structure stripers need to ambush bait.

The best striper fishing from a jetty is usually at night. Stripers may not feel safe in the shallow water near shore when the sun is high, but will come in after dark or on overcast days.

The first place to seek stripers along a jetty is right in the rocks. They will graze along the structure in hopes of surprising a meal hiding there. Crabs, worms, small baitfish, and even flounder or tog all become prey to the marauding striper.

To fish close to the structure takes some amount of patience and skill. The learning process will be expensive, as the student will leave a good deal of tackle behind. Once the skill is mastered the tackle expense will diminish, but it never completely balances out to zero.

The way to fish a rock jetty is to make a short cast into the current and close the bail or engage the reel immediately. The lure should not be more than 10 feet from the shore, and as the current bounces it along the rocks the angler must keep a tight line by slowly cranking in slack as the rod tip is raised and lowered. As the lure passes by, the angler may drop the rod tip and bounce the lure a little past his position, but not too far or the rocks will get another meal.

The best lure for this type of fishing is a bucktail or plastic shad because the point of the hook rides up when pressure is on the line.

With the hook pointed up, there is less chance it will find purchase in the rocks. The other problem is the current that can wash the lure into a crevice where it will become lodged. When this happens, you might be able to free the lure by walking upcurrent and pulling it out the way it went in. Of course, if the angler thought he had a strike when the rock ate the lure and he set the hook with gusto, the odds of getting the lure out will not be good, no matter how far back he walks. This sequence is repeated as the angler walks out on the jetty, fishing both sides if possible.

If fishing close is unproductive, change your strategy. Stripers will also cruise just off the jetty looking for a meal that may be washed away from the structure or venture out too far on its own search for food.

To find these stripers, try casting a floating or shallow diving plug and retrieving it slowly back to the rocks. Bomber, Danny, Tsunami, or Cotton Cordell plugs are ideal for this application. One location where stripers are likely to be swimming away from the structure is around the end of the jetty. In most cases there will be rocks or other material spread out in a fan pattern here, either from wave action over the years or from the construction process. These rocks are not visible above the water, but they do hold bait, and this will attract stripers. Work the plug in a fan pattern over the entire area, then go back and do it again.

Jetty stripers seem to come and go more so than the same fish would do over other structures like a rip or shoal. Because of this, anglers might want to work the same area several times during the night, just in case some fish have moved in since you were there the first time.

There is one situation where stripers will take up station at a jetty and stay around for a while. This occurs when the current carries bait past the end of the jetty and the stripers are sitting on the downcurrent side, picking them off. A good example of this is when mullet run down the beach in the fall. Mullet generally stick close to shore, and when they encounter a jetty they will follow it around, often into the waiting mouth of a hungry striper. A darter or one of the mullet-size plugs is deadly in this application. You may also try a popper, as mullet are known to jump when pursued.

Landing any fish from a jetty is a challenge, and a big striper only increases the difficulty factor. I have seen some jetty fishermen try to manage a big net with a long handle, but most use a long-handled gaff. Mine is made from a rod blank with a cork tape handle and a gaff hook secured to the end with waterproof glue. It is about six feet long and will reach out far enough to grab a striper at the base of the rocks.

One alternative to a gaff or net is the Berkley Big Game Lip Grabber. It has a set of clamplike jaws on the end that are opened by pulling on the handle then placed in the striper's mouth and closed by releasing the handle. You need a bit of luck and some cooperation from the fish, but it will do the job.

Every jetty fisherman needs some way to carry his tackle out on the rocks. My first surf bag was a surplus WWII gas mask bag that attached to a WWII web belt. Then I used a canvas surf bag purchased at Johnny's in Montauk. It has aluminum dividers to keep the plugs apart and small pockets on the side for leaders, snaps, and swivels. A few years ago, my oldest son, Ric, gave me a Tals bag that he had found on the Internet. It has plastic tubes that store one or more lures, and the bag opens flat so you can find the tackle you want without digging through a bunch of stuff with sharp hooks. The adjustable straps allow the wearer to carry the bag on his side or on his chest. The side position is great for normal surf fishing and the chest position is good when wading.

A good jetty or surf bag must be well constructed and have plastic or stainless dividers to keep lures and rigs from tangling. The dividers must be sturdy to take the abuse of being thrown on the rocks and otherwise mistreated. In the old days, heavy canvas was the only choice for jetty bag construction, but today there are many light but durable materials on the market and they do exceptionally well when made into surf or jetty bags.

Ease of access is another important point when considering a jetty bag. My old Army gas mask bag was tough, but required a bit of fumbling around to find the gear I was after. My new Tals bag opens flat and each lure or rig is in its own plastic tube. Even my old canvas bag has stainless dividers that make locating a favorite plug easy.

Surf Tackle

Surf tackle takes quite a beating from the elements and the terrain. It will be exposed to salt spray, sand, and rocks, when not riding along on the front of the beach buggy, where road grime will add to the mix. Because of this rough treatment, only high quality tackle will hold up and is the only type I would recommend. You must also take care of the tackle after every trip to the beach. Clean out all the sand and grime, then spray the rod, reel, and line with WD-40 or other water-replacing oil. The oil will leave a residue that will hold fine sand on the tackle, but this is easily removed with a small brush. I would rather brush off some sand and have the protection of the oil than replace my tackle every year.

With so many ways to fish the surf, there is never going to be one rod and reel that will suit every situation. The angler who fishes with plugs will need a light outfit so the constant casting will not wear him out. The guy who tosses a bunker head and an eight-ounce sinker into the surf needs a sturdy stick and a reel that will hold at least 300 yards of heavy line. In between you have the jetty jockey who needs a light but study rod, the light tackle guy who likes to toss small plastics, and all the other variations dictated by personal preference.

I like to use a conventional outfit when tossing big baits and weights. My current outfit of choice for this work is a Tsunami TSTSC 1102XH rod with an Ambassadeur 9000 reel and 50-pound Stren braid. The 9000 does not have a line guide that can get full of sand on the beach. The rod is rated for four to eight ounces, and, while I cannot cast as far as some, I do manage to at least hit the water most of the time.

For lighter bait casting I stick with the same Ambassadeur reel but use the Tsunami TSTSC1002H rod. When tossing plugs or metal, the Tsunami TSCS701H rod and a Jarvis Walker 5500 reel with 30-pound braid is great, and the St. Croix MDS60 rod with an Okuma MDS60 reel and 30-pound Spiderwire is my choice for jetty fishing. Naturally, most major and all custom shops make similar outfits. Some custom shops, like Hatteras Jack's in Rodanthe, North Carolina, will build you a custom rod and reel. Ryan White, the owner, is a world-class long distance caster and has been building rods since his youth.

Most of the time surf fishermen will tie a shock leader on their line to take the abuse of repeated casts. Jetty jockeys benefit from the shock leader because it not only takes the abuse from casting, but also the contact with rocks, mussels, and other obstructions. All shock leaders must be checked while fishing and are usually replaced after every trip.

I use monofilament leader in the 30- to 50-pound range and secure it to the braided line with an Albright knot. Don't forget to use a double Uni-knot when the reel is full of Power Pro braid.

The shocker should be long enough to wrap around the reel at least twice, pass through all the guides and fall back to the first or gathering guide. By doing this, the knot will be on the reel when casting and the shock leader will be back on the reel when trying to wrestle the fish through the breakers or drag it up the beach.

Since most surf fishing for stripers is done at night, a good headlamp is a must. Mine is from Streamlite, and it is bright, yet as light as possible. The light has three bulbs: green, white, and very bright.

Waders are a must when striper fishing, even in the summer, because the fish prefer colder water that can quickly chill a fisherman. At the least, most of us will wear a set of foul weather gear, unless the night is particularly warm. In my experience, if the water is warm enough to wade in wearing shorts, the probability of catching a good striper is quite low.

One factor that must be emphasized is safety. Fishing the surf at night is dangerous, and if you fall into the waves chances are good that you won't come back up. Wear a pullover foul weather jacket over the waders and belt it around the waist to prevent the waders from filling with water. Maybe wear a pair of those new suspender PFDs, although they are somewhat expensive. I have fished the surf for over 50 years and have been knocked down more than once by a wave I did not see. It can happen to anyone and always at the worst time.

The selection of lures for striper fishing in the surf is endless. I have enough to stock a small tackle shop and fish with guys that have even more.

On a recent trip to Cuttyhunk, Massachusetts, I carried a very large duffel bag stuffed with tackle, while several of my companions did the same. Also along was a novice surf caster who borrowed a rod and reel from me and fished the entire week with the one surface popper he owned. He caught more and bigger fish than anyone else, not because of his tackle, but because he was willing to walk three miles to and from his hot spot, swim and wade across a tidal creek, and climb out on the rocks when he got there. I would not have felt so bad if he had been 20 years old, but he is 65, two years older than me.

A selection of surf and jetty lures.

In my collection of striper lures for the surf are a Stan Gibbs bottle plug, several Atom Juniors, a Gibb's darter, Danny plugs, Bombers, and a good supply of Atom, Creek Chub Striper Strike, Tsunami, Yo-Zuri, and Storm poppers. I keep several Hopkins lures at the ready and will usually decorate them with a six-inch white plastic worm. Point Judith has brought back the tin squid in several shapes and sizes, along with some very good eel imitations. The plastic shads from Berkley, Tsunami, Storm, and others have become staples, as have the smaller plastics from Lunker City, Tsunami, and Mann's.

Many surf fishermen carry a short gaff attached to their belt, with a cord similar to the one on a telephone. This can be a great help when landing a big striper in the wash, but would be illegal in states where gaffing stripers is forbidden. A short Boga Grip or a Big Game Lip Grabber from Berkley will also work, but does take a bit of skill or luck and some cooperation from the striper to get the grip part in his mouth.

Working the Beach

Now that we have the tackle and know how to read the beach, it is time to go fishing. I always believe the best time to fish is when you have time to go fishing, but success really depends upon planning your trip to coincide with the best area for the tide you will be fishing. In other words, you can't change the tide cycle, but you can choose the location where you will be fishing. As an example, if the tide is flooding, a shallow beach may produce; on the ebb, look for a beach with a runout or the ocean side of an inlet. Keep in mind that the best action in the surf is usually at night or at dawn or dusk.

A surf and jetty bag must offer enough capacity for a proper selection of lures.

Fishing an open sand beach with no rocks, wrecks, or other hard structure is more like hunting than fishing. The angler may walk along the beach casting in a fan pattern with different lures until he locates some action. He may also choose to stay in one place, fishing a break in the bar or a runout, waiting for the stripers to move in range.

Begin with a long cast and a slow retrieve, working the lure right to the beach. Stripers will occasionally follow the lure almost to the sand before striking, so don't pull it out of the water too soon.

Plastic jigs are a good bet in the surf.

Start with a Danny or Bomber and then go to a bucktail or plastic shad to cover the whole water column. As always, use a very slow retrieve, even with the jigs. Jigs should be bounced across the bottom, keeping just enough pressure on the line to maintain contact with the lure.

Rock beaches are fished much the same way as sand beaches. The advantage here is the presence of larger rocks close to the beach. Cast to these rocks when available, or just work the beach as if it were sand. Using bucktails, plastic shads, or other jigs can be a challenge over rocks, but by carefully feeling the bottom through the line you can keep the lure from hanging up.

Poppers come into play during the day when you are prospecting for stripers. Cast them out as far as possible and then retrieve them with sufficient action to attract the striper's attention. Getting a hit on a popper in the surf is one of the great thrills in fishing, and once attracted to the noise, stripers will usually keep after the lure until they feel a hook. Keep working the popper until the striper is on or gone.

If there is a submerged rock or any other hard structure in the surf, work the popper as close to it as possible. Such structure often holds stripers, but they stay tight and a lure must pass right by their nose to be attractive.

I have recently heard of anglers having success with surface lures at night. This is something I have not tried, but is certainly worth a shot.

Lure color is something that can start an argument on any beach. I have found yellow, white, green, and blue all work during the day and I stick with black at night. If you have luck fishing a pink polka-dot, electric blue back swimmer then do not change your choice on my account.

All casting in the surf is dictated by the beach structure and the weather conditions. A point may produce well as the current sweeps past the end on the flood, while the deep slough between the beach and an outer bar may hold stripers as the waves wash over the bar and into the deeper water. You must read the beach and know where and how to fish it on every stage of the tide.

Bucktails are a standard surf bait that will work on any stage of the tide.

Unless the current is dead slack, there will be movement up and down the beach depending on the direction of the current. Along east-facing beaches on the East Coast, the current will move north on the incoming and south on the outgoing. This means if a lure is cast out 90 degrees from the angler's position, it will move to the left on the flood and to the right on the ebb. Along south-facing beaches, the sweep will be east on the flood and west on the ebb. The current will be stronger on a full or new moon and fall off as the moon wanes and fills. When the wind and current are in harmony, the sweep will intensify, and when they oppose each other, the water will be rough and possibly dirty.

The weather conditions in the surf can become a bit difficult, of course. The ideal situa-

A rough surf may be difficult to fish, but big stripers are often caught during bad weather.

tion will be a light onshore breeze that pushes bait close to shore and has the water nice and clean. Sometimes that nice onshore breeze blows 20 to 30 and the waves reach 8 to 10 feet, making it all but impossible to fish, at least to fish with any semblance of safety.

An offshore wind generally drops the water temperature in the surf and pushes the bait further away from the beach. On the plus side, we all cast like champions with the wind to our backs. This is the time to fish that far outer bar, where the stripers may be picking off baitfish washed over by the waves.

There will be times when the weather is marginal. The wind may be 10 to 15 miles per hour onshore, with five- to six-foot waves and a lot of roiled water in the wash. While dif-

ficult to fish, these are the conditions that attract big stripers. Break out the heavy tackle, the big plugs, and cast right into the teeth of the wind. When that 50-pounder hits you will know you have earned her.

The presence of baitfish is another factor in determining what and when to fish. Mullet are long, thin fish with very dark backs that almost always travel close to the beach in tight schools on the surface. Bunker come in all sizes from peanut to large and are silver with a broad, flat profile. They may be on the surface or close to the bottom. Sand eels are long, thin, and silver. They will try to bury in the sand, but will also travel in schools along the beach. Other surf baits include herring, shad, silversides, rainfish, anchovies, and small bluefish or weakfish. Mullet schools are usually long, with the fish spread out, showing as ripples on the surface. Bunker schools will show as dark areas, with the occasional fish breaking the surface. Rainfish, spearing, and other small bait can often be seen jumping out of the water, especially when disturbed by a lure or even the line.

Once the type of baitfish in the area has been established, the angler should choose a lure to match the forage. Sweetwater fly fishermen call it matching the hatch, and while they are talking about bugs, the same idea applies to baitfish.

The one condition that frustrates all surf fishing is the presence of weeds. It is all but impossible to fish when your plug is covered in weeds as soon as it hits the water. Even bait fishing is difficult when the line loads up and drags the bait ashore. I can put up with a few weeds, but when they cover line, lure, and terminal tackle in a matter of seconds, I pack it in for that tide.

The water will usually be full of weeds after an onshore blow that has flooded the marshes, picking up all the grass and weeds that have been covering the ground. Eelgrass can build up along the shoreline and will be carried back out when the tide is high during a storm or on a full or new moon.

Getting On the Beach

Beach access varies from forbidden territory to wide open, with most falling somewhere between. The majority of beaches can be fished by walk-ons because the surf line is common property, but getting across private property to reach the surf line can be problematic. Fortunately, there are many areas along the coast with good public access, and this is where anglers should concentrate their efforts.

Walk-on fishermen usually carry one rod and a surf bag full of tackle as they ply the surf. They may depart from a deserted parking lot on Assateague Island or a crowded street in Asbury Park where they must fill the parking meter.

With the best surf action after dark, few anglers encounter any bathers; however, the occasional couple enjoying the solitude of a lonely beach may be seen. Just walk past and try not to watch. While not a common occurrence, I have heard stories of surf fishermen being mugged in some urban locations, so it pays to stay on your guard.

Fishing the surf during the day from a public beach is possible once the water cools to the low 50s in the fall. Stripers seem to work in close with less apprehension then, and daytime blitzes are not uncommon.

Most often the walk from the parking lot to the water is reasonably short, but there are a few places where a Sherpa guide would find the trek challenging. One of these is Sandy Point, New Jersey, where the point is well over a mile from the parking lot. Another is the point on Cape Hatteras; however, only a few walk out here because the area is open to surf fishing vehicles.

One of the top walk-on surf spots is Pea Island just south of Oregon Inlet on Hatteras Island. Erosion has washed away much of the beach here and driving on the beach is not permitted. The same erosion has brought the surf line close to and occasionally over the road, so anglers have a very short walk to some of the best beach structure along the East Coast. In fact, an angler can drive down the road and spot birds working in the surf on the other side of the dunes.

Driving on the beach does allow for more exploration as well as a much easier way to get your gear to the surf. This is convenience for some and a necessity for those of us of a certain age. Each area where driving on the beach is permitted has a separate set of rules and regulations. Most charge some type of fee, with the Outer Banks of North Carolina one of the few beaches open to all for free.

I began my beach driving in 1973 with a 1971 International Scout. My first trip to Hatteras put me in the middle of a big bluefish blitz just south of the point, and I have been hooked ever since. My poor old Scout finally got very tired, and I bought a 1987 Dodge Ramcharger with a V8 and automatically locking wheel hubs. After all those years of driving the beach in low range, it was pure joy to have the power to stay in high. After 13 years and well over 150,000 miles, the Ramcharger made way for a Chevy Avalanche with an 8.1-liter engine and enough power to go anywhere. We won't talk about the gas mileage, but I do get Christmas cards every year from several Arab sheiks.

Few of us can afford a surf fishing vehicle that only sees duty on the beach. At the very least we will drive it to work every day and at the most it will be the only family car. With this in mind, you'll learn to separate the fishing stuff from the day-to-day stuff. The new lines of 4WD vehicles from manufacturers as diverse as Porsche and Kia have plenty of storage space, with seating for the entire family. Still, no one wants a smelly bait cooler in the same compartment as their family, so cooler and rod racks are commonplace on today's surf vehicles. Some, like my Avalanche, are able to close off the back from the front so we can keep our tackle on board while ferrying people around. Other pickup trucks use a cap or have a cover over the cargo space where surf fishing equipment can be stored.

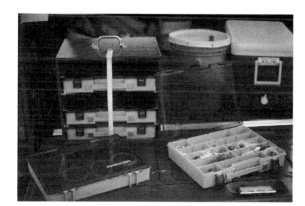

Careful tackle storage will make finding what you need much easier, especially at night.

The one thing I have found very useful when equipping my truck for surf fishing is those small plastic tackle boxes available from many manufacturers. I can set them up for school stripers in the spring, jetty fishing in the

summer, and the big girls that visit in the fall and only take the boxes I need at any given time. They are also great for fishing from the boat for the same reasons.

New beach drivers must learn to let the air out of their tires before going out to the sand. Each vehicle will be a bit different depending on its weight and type of tires. The type of sand on the beach is also a factor, with fine, soft sand requiring lower tire pressure than the hard-packed stuff. Of course, you can encounter both types on the same beach. I would try something between 15 and 20 pounds in each tire to begin with, and if you find you can get away with the higher end of the scale, fine. Just remember, the lower tire

An arsenal of surf fishing equipment rests during midday while its owners recover from the predawn expedition and prepare for the night tides.

pressure will get you through the unexpected soft spot.

Please behave yourself when driving on the beach. Stay off the dunes, don't speed, know when and how to give the right of way on the rutted driving lanes, keep a close eye out for pedestrians, dogs, kids, and, sometimes, even people on horseback. And whatever you do, don't get stuck, because the cost of a tow job off the beach will really hurt the tackle budget. Take shovels to dig your way out, just in case.

Seven

Fly Fishing

The resurgence of striped bass along the East Coast has renewed the interest in saltwater fly fishing. Because stripers spend so much time close to structure and in relatively shallow water, they are the perfect targets for the fly caster. I am not what anyone would call an accomplished fly caster, and the fact that I have actually caught stripers on a fly proves how easy it is.

If you are interested in saltwater fly fishing, do not let the idea that it is expensive keep you from trying. In today's world there are good saltwater fly-fishing outfits with reasonable

A standard fly rod when fishing for stripers.

price tags, and, while the more expensive models bring the prestige that some anglers find more important than function, the less expensive models will catch just as many fish. As I once told a custom rod builder who was making fun of my surf stick with the cork tape handle and the reel held on by black electrical tape, the day a fish swims up onshore to check out my equipment before biting my bait is the day I would purchase his most expensive model.

If you watch those television shows where fly casters throw a fly 80 feet to spooky bonefish on a crystal clear Florida flat, you may think all fly fishermen must cast that far. Believe me, if that were true, I would never have caught a striper on a fly. Just like surf fishing, fly fishing

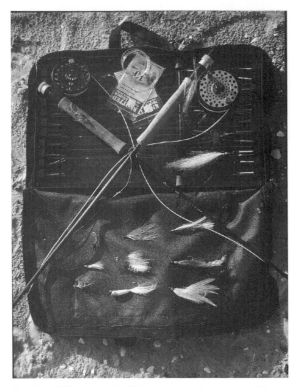

A striper fisherman's fly fishing bag and related tackle.

Many striper fly fishermen work from the beach. Here the wind will always be in your face and even a 100-foot cast may not reach beyond the breakers. Fortunately, stripers will be right in the wash, and while the big guns with their Hatteras Heavers, bunker heads, and 300-foot casts are hauling water, the fly caster can be catching stripers right in the wash.

I have heard stories about Joe Brooks, who was said to be the best long distance caster in recent times, casting great distances in horrible conditions. Joe died before I had a chance to meet him, but I have taken fly casting lessons from one of his students, the great Lefty Kreh, who had me making 60- to 70-foot casts after only a few minutes of instruction. If I had continued to practice the methods he taught, I am sure I would be casting over 100 feet today. Such was not the case, but if you are serious about fly casting in salt water, I highly recommend taking lessons. Then practice, practice, practice.

will be more productive the further the angler can cast, but also like surf fishing, most of the time the stripers will be much closer.

As an example, fishing for stripers in a chum slick requires no casting at all. Just let the fly sink with the chunks and it will carry right to the waiting stripers. Fishing around heavy structure like rocks or bridge pilings does not require long casts either. Even casting to breaking stripers, where you want to keep the boat as far away as possible from the action, should not require a cast of more than 50 feet. This is one place where the ability to cast long distances can come in handy, but is not absolutely required. But those who fish for stripers in clear, shallow water must cast long distances in order not to spook the fish.

Casting to bridge pilings.

Tackle

In order to make this as accurate as possible, I have contacted noted experts in the saltwater fly fishing world and asked for their advice on the subject. The first of these experts is Jerry Gomber, who has fly fished the New Jersey coast for many years. Jerry recommends a nine-foot, nine-weight fly rod and a large arbor reel with a very good drag and anti-reverse. Using your hand as a drag and having a single action reel may be more of a challenge, but it will leave you with broken lines and bruised knuckles.

The reel should hold 200 yards of 30-pound backing. Cortland Micron was the standard, but now more anglers are using braided lines. The fly line should be an intermediate or a floater in the surf.

From boats, if targeting smaller fish, you can drop down to an eight-weight on an eight- to eight-and-a-half-foot rod. A smaller reel to match the rod will also have the 30-pound backing. Fly lines can be intermediate or fast sinking. The larger rod can be used from the boat in nasty weather or when large fish are in the area.

Just about all the major fly-rod manufacturers make a product suited to striper fishing. Some notable brands are G. Loomis, Sage, Orvis, Thomas and Thomas, Scott, Winston, and Powell. A more reasonably priced product may be found at St. Croix, Temple Fork Outfitters, and Scientific Anglers. Look for something in the eight-and-a-half to nine-and-a-half-foot range, from an 8-weight for schoolies up to an 11-weight for the big fish.

While the choice of stiffness is somewhat personal, some stiffness is required to cast bulky flies in the ever present wind associated with striper fishing. A graphite blank of moderate to stiff action will do the job. Keep in mind that a stiff blank will be more difficut to cast while a moderate blank will be a good choice for the less expierenced angler.

Reel seats must be made from a corrosion-resistant material and should never be made from wood because it swells in salt water. Even the best materials should be cleaned and oiled after each use in salt water to prevent salt buildup.

As for fly reels, make sure to choose the correct reel for the size line in use. Striper reels need 100 yards of 20- to 30-pound backing. Ross, Tibor, Tioga, Lamson, Bauer, Orvis, Sage and Abel all make striper-fishing fly reels. While many of these reels are expensive, the Pflueger Medalist, at $30, has landed countless stripers. Other moderately priced reels are available from Scientific Anglers, Redington. and STH.

The author proves anyone can catch a striper on a fly.

Striper fishing, unlike freshwater trout angling, requires a fly reel with a drag system. Be sure the reel you choose has a disc drag as opposed to a spring and pawl setup. A large arbor reel will allow the line to be retrieved at a faster rate, handy when the striper decides to run towards you, a not uncommon experience when the angler is wading.

As for leaders, the standard seems to be long for floating lines and short for sinking lines. According to Roy Miller, who fishes with flies in both fresh and salt water, a nine-foot tapered leader is best when casting floating or intermediate lines. A three- to four-foot straight leader is all that is required when fishing with fast sinking lines. The typical tippet will be in the 12- to 20-pound range, depending on the size of the fish expected.

Flies should be selected to match the local bait, just like lures in any form of fishing. Sarah Gardner, from Fly Girl Charters out of Oregon Inlet in North Carolina, recommends a Clouser or Lefty's Deceiver. There is also a Half-And-Half fly made with weighted eyes like a Clouser and a wide body like a Deceiver.

Attend any saltwater fly-fishing show and you will see any number of flies made from epoxy and looking almost identical to the real bait. Shiners, bunker, crabs, anchovies, sand eels, and everything else a striper may eat will be found in these collections.

The crease fly is something relatively new. It too is made from epoxy, but instead of sinking it floats, and when retrieved the fly makes a wake on the surface.

There are all sorts of popping bugs for saltwater fly fishing and they work exactly like poppers cast from spinning or conventional outfits. One thing I have noticed, however, is that the floating flies do not make as big a commotion on the surface as may be needed to attract a strike. This is particularly noticeable in rough water around a rip or close to waves breaking against rocks or a sea wall. A big popper cast in the rough water has a hit every time, while the fly simply does not make enough surface noise to bring in the fish. Of course, the angler can use a much bigger fly, but this raises casting problems.

Another thing I discovered from my days guiding fly-fishing clients is the importance of a fast sinking fly line. I once drove three doctors to a huge school of breaking stripers, and even with my motor shut off and the boat sitting right in the middle of the action, these guys could not buy a fish. And yet the week before, I had taken aboard two other doctors who caught so many stripers they recommended me and my charter boat to these three other guys. Unfortunately, they forgot to tell the second crew to bring a fast sinking line. The fish were breaking on the surface, but feeding on the bottom. My trio of fly casters had intermediate lines, and they just could not reach the action. I took my conventional outfit, sent a Stingsilver to the bottom, and hooked up on every drop.

When I asked the fly casters if they wanted to try the metal lure on my outfit, they acted as if I had asked them to sell their children. Total score at the end of the day: fly casters, nothing; conventional guy, more than he could count.

In a reverse of that situation, I have had fly fishermen out when the stripers wanted a very small bait presented close to the rock islands of the Chesapeake Bay Bridge Tunnel. On this particular day, my WindCheaters picked at the fish, while the fly guys had stripers on every cast.

On a particularly frustrating trip, I had a woman fly fisher out for some big stripers. She could cast a mile, had enough equipment to open an Orvis shop, and she knew how to use it.

I, on the other hand, knew where the big bass were feeding. We headed for the spot and conditions were perfect: a strong-running current with a nice rip over a drop in the bottom from 10 or 12 feet down to 30 or so. Getting that deep should not have been a problem for her and I am positive she was in the strike zone. Still, no matter how many different flies she tried and how hard I worked to put her over the fish, we never caught a single striper. Meanwhile, friends of mine fishing with 3½-Drones on wire line were catching 30- to 40-inch stripers on every pass. Later in the day we came back in closer to shore and she had 18- to 24-inch stripers on every cast over a similar rip. I have no idea why the bigger fish would not strike the fly; it remains one of the many mysteries of my striper fishing experience.

Once you are outfitted with the proper equipment and learn how to use it, fly fishing is no different than any other type of striper fishing. You must find the fish, make a natural presentation, and put enough pressure on the striper to get him to the boat or beach. You will find many books and even more experts willing to teach you the fine points of catching stripers on the fly. Sort through them carefully, especially the "experts," and learn what you can from each. But once you've got a decent cast going, you'll learn the most from your own fishing.

Eight

When and Where

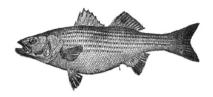

Stripers have a certain pattern they follow, be it along the Atlantic, Gulf, or West coasts. Even freshwater stripers move around their impoundments as the seasons change. We are going to look at these movements specific to a number of places, with suggestions on when and where the angler may intercept his quarry.

Springtime Spawning Run

The Chesapeake Bay supplies most of the Atlantic coast stock, so we will begin by looking at the striper's movements from the time they arrive on the spawning grounds during the spring.

Susquehanna Flats

The first open season for Chesapeake Bay stripers comes in March, when a catch-and-release season opens on the Susquehanna Flats at the head of the bay in Maryland. There has been some controversy about this season, with the more conservative fishermen opposed to targeting stripers when they are on the spawning grounds. On the other hand, the Maryland

Upper bay stripers can be large during the spring run.

THE ULTIMATE GUIDE TO STRIPED BASS FISHING

Department of Natural Resources monitors the catch-and-release season and so far they have not found anything to make them close the season.

The area where catch-and-release fishing is permitted is relatively small when compared to the entire Chesapeake Bay. It is bordered on the north by a line from the railroad bridge at the mouth of the Susquehanna River and on the south by a line from Sandy Point to Turkey Point. Most of the action takes place somewhere along the channels that run up the east and west sides of the flats. Stripers will also be taken in the shallows over and around grass beds.

The preferred technique is to cast surface lures to likely striper hot spots, with the hope of having a big cow crash the plug. This method does not always work, and anglers will switch to Rat-L-Traps, MirrOlures, plastic shads, bucktails, and plastic worms.

In order for any lure to work on the flats, the water has to be clear and warm. By warm, we mean in the 50-degree range. Unfortunately, this is not always the case. The flats were formed by sediment carried down the Susquehanna River and deposited at the head of the bay. The Conowingo Dam now controls the flow from the river, and quite often in the spring heavy rains as far north as New York will require the dam to open the floodgates, allowing cold and dirty water to inundate the flats. When this occurs many anglers give up on fishing, but a few will switch to bait, with cut herring chunks a favorite. Once again, the more conservative anglers decry this practice, claiming it is only used by guides who don't want to lose money and don't care about the stripers. Most of the guides I know use circle

hooks to make the release of their party's catch quick and easy, and all care greatly about the stripers.

This is a small boat fishery because of the shallow water, but it can get nasty on the flats without much notice. You won't see many 10- to 12-foot waves, but if the wind comes up above 10 to 15 knots, there will be enough four-footers to make the trip back to the dock an exciting experience.

Most trailer boaters will launch at Havre De Grace at the mouth of the Susquehanna River, while others will put over at Turkey Point at the mouth of the Elk River. The run from Turkey Point is a bit longer and requires navigating around the point, which can get rough on a hard south wind. Crowds at both launch ramps will be large, especially on warm and sunny weekends. A Maryland, Potomac River, or Virginia saltwater fishing license is required to fish anywhere on the Chesapeake Bay.

Trophy Season

The trophy season is the next to open in Maryland. This will be sometime in early April, and the limit is one striper per angler per day, with a minimum size of 32 inches. The exact dates for all seasons are set each year and may be different from the previous year. Only the open bay is available for trophy fishing. All tributaries are closed to any type of striper fishing, including catch-and-release. The catch-and-release season on the flats may overlap the trophy season.

Like the catch-and-release season, the trophy season has been criticized by some fishermen. They feel targeting stripers who may or may not have spawned is a bad idea. Once again the Maryland DNR has set these seasons

decades, with umbrella rigs armed with plastic shads becoming more popular every year. Smaller lures are saved for later in the season when the minimum size drops to 18 inches and the bag limit is two fish.

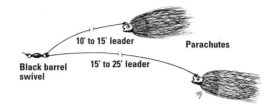

A double parachute rig.

Boat captains troll along channel edges from well above the Bay Bridge at Annapolis to the Virginia line. Tilghman Island has become a popular jumping-off spot for trophy season stripers because boats can cover more productive territory closer to the dock. On the western shore, Chesapeake Beach and Breezy Point are great favorites. In the upper bay, Rock Hall has been a striper departure spot for many years. With improved water quality and a resurgence of homes and marinas along the waterfront, even the city of Baltimore has gotten into the act.

Stripers seem to follow the edge of the channel and do not stage in any one location during the trophy season. Most of the boats will continue to troll up and down the edge picking up stripers as they follow the channels on the way to the ocean.

Open Season

Once the trophy season closes, the tributaries will open, and smaller fish become the target. Chumming, casting, and trolling all become regularly used techniques. Most of the larger

This Chesapeake Bay trophy striper fell to an umbrella rig.

to target stripers after they have finished spawning, and so far they have no evidence that the trophy season is causing great harm to the population.

A single parachute rig.

Trolling is the primary method for taking stripers during the trophy season. Big bucktails and spoons have been used on stripers for

A Chesapeake Bay trolling outfit.

Menhaden chum is used during the Maryland open season.

grounds are popular with boats out of Point Lookout and Smith Island. The Chinese Mud is close to Solomon's Island, as are the Gas Docks. Boats out of Tilghman Island, Chesapeake Beach, and Deal Island may chum on Holland Bar or the Stone Rock. Above the Bay Bridge, Love Point, Pool's Island, and Tolchester Reef are just a few of the places where chumming is practiced.

Small-boat guides will try to take their stripers by casting with either lures or flies. They work the shallow near-shore areas, the rivers and sheltered bays. Eastern Bay is a favorite along with the shallows out of Crisfield.

These small-boat guides are very flexible and can fish anywhere along both the Eastern and Western shore. Light tackle and fly fishing is their specialty, with good success on most trips from spring to late fall.

Trailer boaters can accomplish the same thing by moving up and down the bay along with the movement of the stripers. There are launch ramps in just about every waterfront town, and local tackle shops will be happy to share information on where the fish have been and what they were hitting.

The trailer boat fisherman is not limited to what technique he uses, and many will troll, chum, and cast all in the same day. The day may begin with casting to schools of stripers on the surface, then trolling umbrella rigs after the fish go down, and finally setting up to chum at a favorite location. The one thing he can count on is plenty of company wherever he decides to fish.

Virginia

Maryland anglers are fortunate to have a striper season that runs from early spring until

charter boats chum because it is the most user-friendly technique. Some will troll early in the day, targeting whatever big stripers are left, but if that is not successful they will get in the chumming fleet. The Southwest Middle the end of the year. In Virginia, the first season will begin on May 1, when only trophy stripers are fair game. This will run until May 15, when the spring season begins and anglers are allowed two fish between 18 and 28 inches.

For some reason the trophy season does not attract a lot of attention. There will be boats trolling the channel edges from the Maryland line all the way to the Chesapeake Bay Bridge Tunnel, but not in any great numbers. Others will try wire line or live bait over the tunnel tubes.

Once the spring season opens, interest will increase, but with flounder, trout, bluefish, red drum, black drum, and the possibility of an early season cobia, anglers may not spend too much time on the slot limit stripers.

My personal favorite is casting to the rocks at the base of the four islands that support the two tunnels. I begin in the morning with surface lures, then switch to plugs as the sun comes up. Fly casters do equally well in this area.

Charter boats, head boats, and private craft will pull larger fish by dropping live bait over the tunnel tubes. Croaker is the best choice for this action. Because there are so many different fish available during the spring season, many anglers will catch a quick limit of stripers in the morning then move on to other species later in the day.

Bait fishing with fresh clams, bunker, or peeler crabs accounts for a good number of spring stripers, but not because they were the original target. These baits are set out for red or black drum and the stripers join the party without an invitation.

The spring season will end on June 15, and the fall season will not open until October 4. This season generates a lot more excite-ment, as stripers over 32 inches may be retained. The current regulations for the fall season allow two fish between 18 and 28 inches or one fish between 18 and 28 inches and one over 32 inches.

Atlantic Coast of Virginia and Maryland

Striper fishing along the Atlantic coast of Virginia and Maryland is completely different than the seasons in the Chesapeake Bay. The limit here is two stripers per day, with a minimum size of 28 inches.

The Virginia ocean coast is difficult to fish because most of it is not accessible by car. The Barrier Islands of Virginia are unmolested beaches primarily because the Nature Conservancy purchased many of them in the 1970s and 80s. The Conservancy has prevented construction on the islands and all are currently uninhabited.

This does not mean you can't fish here. The islands are open to the public if the public is willing to go out there in a small boat. Most of the public is not so inclined.

The Conservancy does have strict rules governing the use of the islands, so check with them before heading out. There are numerous launch ramps along the sea side of the Eastern Shore of Virginia. The ones in Gargatha, Wachapreague, Quinby, and Oyster are popular with surf fishermen.

When fishing the Virginia surf in the spring, cut fresh bait or peeler crabs are the top baits. Clams are also effective, but do not stay on the hook well, especially when the water is rough.

When I began fishing the Barrier Islands, the spring target was red drum. We soaked peeler crabs in the surf and never thought about catching striped bass. That was in the 1970s and things have changed. Today we still fish for red drum, but we catch more than a few stripers.

The only section of Virginia Beach open to vehicles is the southern part of Assateague Island adjacent to Chincoteague. It is about a mile and a half long and does produce the occasional striper.

In spite of the trolling that goes on in the Chesapeake Bay, few anglers troll the coastal waters in the spring. This will change dramatically in the fall.

The north end of Assateague Island in the spring is a center for striper-hungry surf fishermen. They will pay $70 to the National Park Service and receive a permit to drive the Maryland portion of the island from one end to the other looking for good water. Once you choose a location, you play a waiting game as peeler crab, cut bunker, and bloodworms are soaked awaiting the arrival of the stripers. The number of stripers caught here is not real high, but the size is generally large. The best action is at night or on overcast days.

Ocean City, Maryland receives some attention from surf fishermen during the spring. The same technique as used on Assateague is employed here, with the exception of driving on the beach.

The Ocean City Inlet and the Route 50 Bridge will see striper activity from spring until winter. Anglers will use more lures here than on the surf, with plastic shads and bucktails the top choices. Live eels are soaked from both locations, with the best action on night tides.

Delaware Bay and Coast

Spring-run stripers will show up off the Delaware coast sometime in April. Surf fishermen soak bunker heads from Fenwick Island to Cape Henlopen and land a few big fish. Inside Indian River Inlet all the way up to Oak Orchard, anglers fish with bloodworms, and while most of the catch will be under the 28-inch minimum size, there will be a few big fish taken. There is a small breeding stock in the river that provides the big cows in the spring.

The real action begins in Delaware Bay. This is a somewhat unusual situation because the bay receives stripers from several directions. Some of the Chesapeake Bay stock will enter the upper bay through the Chesapeake and Delaware Canal. There is a small spawning stock in the bay, with females arriving through the C&D Canal as well as from the ocean. The lower bay will receive stripers migrating along the Atlantic coast. For these reasons there are stripers available to fishermen from as far up the Delaware as Trenton and as far south as Lewes and Cape May.

Beginning in the upper bay, anglers will line the banks along both the Delaware and New Jersey sides soaking bloodworms and cut bait. The fishing is usually on the slow side, but patience can be rewarded with a big striper.

Chunking from a boat anchored on structure is a more productive method. The Yellow Can, the pilings at the Delaware Memorial Bridge, the Pipes, and along the Pea Patch Island breakwater are all good locations to chunk. Most of the bigger stripers are caught on bunker heads fished right on the bottom. The launch ramp at Augustine Beach in Delaware is a popular place to depart.

The bait for both chumming and bank fishing will be cut bunker. In the spring, fresh bunker may not be available, so frozen will have to do. Both groups also use bloodworms.

If the stripers stay around until the first crab molt, peelers become a very popular bait.

On the Jersey side of the Delaware River and the upper bay, the mouths of creeks and even back up in the creek a way become popular places to catch a big striper in the spring. Jim Hutchinson, a lifelong New Jersey resident, recommends the Penns Grove and Fortescue beaches or Graveling Point in Tuckerton for early season striper action. When I did the South Jersey fishing reports for the *New Jersey Fisherman* magazine, Forked River was a good spring location. Here too the action will be a bit slow, but trophies show up every year. Bloodworms are the most popular bait on the Jersey side, with cut bunker and shedder crab used as well.

The Delaware side has two free state-run fishing piers that provide good action on stripers. The Woodland Beach pier was constructed in 2005 and has been good for stripers since it opened. Fishermen work from here both day and night using everything from cut bunker to bucktails. The pier at Port Mahon is a bit more rustic, but it too has fans that find striper fishing best on the flood tide.

Out in the Delaware Bay, drifting with live eels at Brown Shoal is the most popular method in the spring. Stripers gobble eels as they move down the bay after the spawn, with most of the action occurring during the day. Cedar Creek at Slaughter's Beach is the closest ramp on the Delaware side, while Fortescue is the best jumping off location on the Jersey side.

The 14-Foot Light and an abandoned lighthouse known as the Flattop are popular with anglers who like to toss bucktails and other such lures. The majority of fish taken here are under the 28-inch minimum size, but

Live eels are the favorite bait of Delaware Bay striper fishermen.

the occasional keeper does make an appearance. Slaughter's or Bowers Beaches are close to these structures.

The Cape May Rips at the mouth of the bay will hold migrating spring stripers for a while, and the fleet will be drifting eels through the schools. This may be the most frequented location, as all the stripers that come to Delaware Bay, be it through the C&D Canal, the resident spawning stock, or the coastwide migration, must pass by. Launch ramps at Lewes, Delaware, and Cape May, New Jersey, see most of the boats heading to the rips.

New Jersey Coast

As the spring migration of stripers moves north, it passes the coast of New Jersey, and that state's numerous anglers turn out to meet them. Surf fishermen from Cape May to Sandy Hook soak bloodworms, clams, and cut bunker for countless hours in hopes of attracting a cow. The shore along Long Beach Island is very popular with reasonably easy access. In Raritan, the boaters chum with clams or bunker on inshore shoals, lumps, and rocks.

Bay clams are the preferred bait as boats line up off of Sandy Hook on the running tide. Some open the clams at the dock before leaving, while others open them after they start fishing and use the shells as chum. Hook the clam through the foot to let it move along the bottom with the current. You'll have quite a thrill cranking in stripers within sight of the New York skyline.

Boaters out of Shark River or Manasquan might choose to chum with bunker or with clams. The anglers toss the chunks and then fish the head or other body parts, dropping it back in the current.

Mojos produce big stripers in May.

Beginning in May, big bunker show up along the coast, and trolling with bunker spoons or Mojos is very productive. Find the bunker schools and you will find the stripers.

New York

The next springtime stop for the migrating stripers is New York. Here and in northern New Jersey, the coastal stock meets up with the Hudson River stock. Tagging studies have shown that the Hudson River stock remains, for the most part, between the mouth of the river and the north end of the Long Island Sound. Of course, some of these fish will join the coastal migration and some migrating stripers will spend the summer in Long Island Sound.

According to Chas Stamm, Director of the Hudson River Fishermen's Association, there is a resident striper population in the Hudson River, but the springtime is when the big females from the coastal stock arrive, and fishermen take notice. Most anglers use sandworms or cut bunker fished on the bottom. A few anglers troll with spoons and plugs. One good location to catch a large fish is the Liberty State Park in New Jersey. In New York, try Englewood Boat Basin and the Alpine Boat Basin within the Palisades Interstate Park. The Piermont Pier is another good springtime fishing spot.

New York striper season currently opens in April, but in most years the best of the spring run won't get rolling until May. By now we are far enough north that some of the migrating stripers will stick around all summer.

Just about every bait used in every other area is used in New York. Live bunker, eels, clams, crabs, small blues, porgies, and worms are some of the most popular. Bait will be the best bet during the spring, with lures used more during the summer and fall.

Almost any place on Long Island with access to the ocean or Long Island Sound will have striper action from shore or from a boat. There are guides, head, and charter boats available for everything from bottom bouncing with jigs to fly fishing. Every time I fish Long Island, I have to remind myself that one of the largest cities in the world is only a few miles away. Actually, I am reminded of that while coming to or leaving the island on the Long Island Expressway.

Bridges attract a lot of attention from Long Island anglers. Some are fished from the structure itself, while others are worked from boats.

One of the best of the New York bridge fishermen was the late Al Reinfelder. He was the man who, along with Lou Palma, invented the bait tail that has evolved into the plastic jig we all use today. Al would chart the tides at different bridges and use the subway system to fish each one at the most productive time.

These tube lures work well around bridges after dark.

Bridge fishing is best done at night when the bait gathers along the light line. The bait tail or other plastic jig is worked along this line, where it may be seen by a hungry striper. Like many special techniques in striper fishing, this one requires a good deal of local knowledge and quite a few sleepless nights to perfect.

I have heard numerous stories of bridge fishermen eluding the police when fishing or parking in prohibited locations. Another story tells of a bridge fisherman who was hiding under the railing when he said something to a passerby and about scared the poor guy to death. It takes all kinds of people to make up the striper fishing clan.

More and more Long Island fishermen are taking advantage of the abundant stripers and the clear water in the shallows to do some sight fishing. This has been compared to bonefishing the southern flats, as the stripers are hunted from shallow draft boats before the angler casts a fly or other lure. The area around Orient Point on the North Shore is becoming famous for this activity.

One of the most easily accessed places to fish is the Shinnecock Canal. It is open to fishing all year both day and night and produces stripers along with just about everything else in New York's salt water. Three locks open and close on a regular schedule to control the water flow through the canal, matching the water levels between the North and South Shores. According to Tom Melton, a Long Island fishing guide and outdoor writer, the best times to fish the canal are during periods when the locks are closed. A 45-minute period after the gates open is also productive, but during times of maximum current flow, working a bait or lure is difficult. I was here with Tom one night when there were high wind warnings all over the island and we were able to fish, although we failed to connect with a striper. I caught a couple of weakfish and Tom had a sea robin or two on plastic jigs.

New England

Now we have arrived at the place where the coastal striper migration spreads out to spend the summer. They will travel all the way up to Maine, and some may even cross into Canada waters, where they could meet up with a spawning population from the several rivers. By this time there will be stripers from as far south as the Roanoke River mixed with the Chesapeake Bay, Delaware Bay, Hudson River, and other stocks from lesser spawning rivers making up the migration.

For the most part, the coastal population is composed of females, with a few males mixed in either from the local spawning areas or those that decided to do some traveling with all those lovely females. This means that New England is the best place to catch a big striper during the summer, and, as history has shown, it is a pretty good place to catch an even bigger fish in the fall.

Charles Church caught a 73-pound striper on a rigged eel while trolling from a rowboat off of Cuttyhunk Island in August of 1913. That record stood until Bob Rocchetta landed a 76-pounder on July 17, 1981. He was drifting an eel off of Montauk Point during a lunar eclipse.

There have been more bass over 60 pounds caught from New England waters than any other location, but the current world record came from Atlantic City, New Jersey, on July 21, 1982. Al McReynolds caught this 78-pound, 8-ounce striper on a Rebel Wind-Cheater plug during a hard northeast blow.

At that time I was doing the South Jersey Report for the *New Jersey Fisherman* magazine, and when McReynolds checked his fish in at Campbell Marine they called me to come over and record the event. I was living in Newark, Delaware, about two hours from Atlantic City, so I called my editor, Pete Barrett, who was in Bricktown, and he went down and took the photos.

There has been much discussion about the possibility of Mr. McReynolds' record being broken, and I feel that it certainly will be in the not too distant future. The great year classes in the Chesapeake Bay have produced an abundance of stripers, and once they reach 15 to 20 years of age, there will be a few that will weigh above 78 pounds. Keep in mind that these fish were born in the 1990s and none will reach 15 years of age until 2008. Once that happens, it is only a matter of time before someone breaks the record. We are already seeing more 60-pounders at this writing.

Summer

Striper fishing in the summer will be on the top of the list for northern anglers, while their counterparts to the south will not pursue them with the same vigor. Once the spring run is over, the southern areas will hold predominantly small stripers, and with the exception of Maryland's portion of the Chesapeake Bay, where the minimum size is only 18 inches, interest in striper fishing will not be great.

Summer in this section of the Chesapeake will find anglers trolling and chumming. The most popular trolling rig is an umbrella with small plastic shads. But even this setup catches many stripers too small to keep, which must be released. The release survival rate is not too good when the water temperature goes above 60 degrees, and while I have seen no studies documenting the mortality of summer-caught stripers, I fear that it is fairly high. On the positive side, many of these stripers are caught on lures, so the possibility of having to release a deep-hooked fish is not common.

With chumming you have the opposite situation. All of these stripers are caught on bait, and while many anglers now use circle hooks, there are so many shorts taken that the mortality rate could be extensive. I have heard charter captains on the bay say that the small stripers are so accustomed to being fed from the stern of the boat that before the captain can set the anchor there will be schools of small fish behind the boat waiting for a handout. I suppose this proves that enough fish survive the catch-and-release process to alter the behavior habits of the entire population. But, again, fishing with bait is best done with circle hooks, and quick releases of nonkeeper fish are a must.

You will find anglers chumming and trolling from Rock Hall to Point Lookout on and over every piece of bottom structure. This has become the basis of the charter and head boat industry in the Maryland section of the bay. Many will chum or troll until they get a limit of stripers, then set up to bottom fish for croaker, spot, or trout.

Along the ocean coast, surf and jetty fishermen stalk the beaches at night, tossing plugs and eels to what they hope will be striper-hiding spots. The coast of New Jersey probably sees more of this activity than anywhere to the south, but Indian River and Ocean City inlets in Delaware and Maryland do have a resident population of night stalkers.

Summer is the time for grass shrimp chumming in the back bays behind the New Jersey barrier islands. Once again we turn to Jim Hutchinson for this information, and he recommends chumming with grass shrimp at Myer's Hole behind Barnegat Light and the sloping holes along Tice's Shoal. The Middle Grounds behind Beach Haven just south of the Little Island Flats by Morrison's, where the water depth quickly drops to 8 or 10 feet, is another good choice.

Fall

No matter how good striper fishing may be in the spring and summer, the fall brings the best action of the year. This is when schools of stripers begin their southern migration from the waters off New England to the winter grounds off the Virginia and North Carolina coasts.

The migration will begin in September along the northern New England coast, as big stripers fill up on bunker and other large bait. The further south they travel, the larger the schools and the faster the action becomes.

Fall striper fishing has spawned many tournaments, but none more famous than the Martha's Vineyard Striper and Bluefish Tournament. This contest runs for several weeks in the fall and attracts anglers from many regions. I went out there to fish in the surf division of the tournament during a New England trip in the 1970s, but to my disappointment, I found access to the beach was very restricted and never wet a line. The tournament also has a boat division, and trolling or casting takes many of the larger fish. The tournament was in progress in 2005 when I paid a visit to Cuttyhunk Island, and we saw several boats working the shoreline and Sow and Pigs Reef trying to catch a winning striper.

My trip to Cuttyhunk in September of 2005 was an education. I had read about the fabulous striper fishing there and was very excited by the prospect of fishing the same waters where Charles Church caught his 73-pounder. Those who remember the fall of '05 will recall that it was very warm, and when we arrived on Cuttyhunk the water temperature was still in the 60s. The air temperature was in the 70s and 80s, and I fished the entire week in shorts. Very comfortable, but not the best striper weather. A hurricane passed by the day we arrived, and we had a beach covered in weeds for most of the week.

I realized very quickly why the early members of the Cuttyhunk Bass Club built piers from the land out past the rock-covered shoreline. Those rocks are covered with slimy marine growth, and walking on them is like walking on a hill covered with ice-encrusted bowling balls. Not the place for old men like me who have bones that break very quickly and heal very slowly.

As you may have already guessed, all of these excuses presage the admission that I had very poor fishing success on Cuttyhunk Island. I caught one striper on a popper late in the afternoon and one on a black Bomber at night.

Another island that I visited in hopes of catching a trophy striper in the surf was Block Island off the coast of Rhode Island. The three days we spent there were the coldest I have experienced and that includes all the time I spent in a Delaware goose pit. The wind came up a gale out of the northwest as soon as we landed, and we were forced to stay an extra day because the ferry could not run. Russ Wilson, whom no one would ever call a sissy, and I never left the house except to go to the restaurant, and we almost froze to death during that short walk. Fred Golofaro and Timmy Coleman did suit up and tried to fish the lee

shore one night, but to no avail. Timmy did catch two stripers over 60 pounds from Block Island, but not on that rip.

Despite my experiences on Block, Cuttyhunk, and Martha's Vineyard, better fishermen than I have recorded some remarkable stripers from those waters. Nantucket is one island that I have not fished and therefore do not have to make any excuses for not catching stripers there. I understand it is a beautiful place, with the best surf fishing action on and along the beach leading to the point. Boaters will find the point and nearby shoals perfect for casting and trolling. Perhaps someday I can visit, bringing my dark cloud and nasty weather to ruin the fishing for everyone while I am there.

New York

The point at Montauk is a short distance by water from Block Island, but is much easier to reach by car. The fall run here can begin in September, but is much better in October and November. The Montauk area has several famous locations where big stripers have been taken.

Under the light at the tip of Montauk is probably the most famous and always the most crowded. I fished here very briefly one night, preferring to leave the area to the more aggressive among us.

The beach at Shagwong is accessible by beach buggy if you have the proper permits. I have fished there with Bob Lick, who was a fair surf fisherman until he packed it in and moved out West. He does make the occasional return to Montauk when he can pull himself away from those Western trout streams. The beaches accessible from the parking lot at

Camp Hero State Park, where Bob and I caught a few winks of sleep when we were not fishing, include Browns, Sewer Pipe, Kings Point, and Caswells. Tom Melton recommends fishing these areas on a falling tide, but claims they will produce on the flood as well.

Boats sailing from Montauk Harbor will catch striped bass on everything from live eels to Diamond jigs. The fleet of charter boats there can fill the bill for whatever way you like to fish.

As a confirmed surf fisherman, I like the beach at Fire Island, where I have fished with Fred Golofaro. In the fall just about everyone is working lures, either in the open surf or in Fire Island Inlet. The bunker, herring, and mullet are on their fall migration coming out of Great South Bay, and the big stripers are waiting for them. You can drive your beach buggy here, but permits are required. The walk-on angler will find parking reasonably close to the surf.

There are launch ramps in the towns along Great South Bay where boaters may put over to fish in the bay or outside Fire Island Inlet. A fee is charged at all the ramps, and some also require a town permit. Drifting with live eels or bunker has been a time-tested technique for boaters working the inlet or ocean.

There are so many locations to fish for fall-run stripers on Long Island that we could write another book on the subject. That is exactly what Tom Melton has done with *Fishing the Long Island Coast*.

New Jersey

Jim Hutchinson and I have had long conversations on the migration patterns of stripers along the Jersey coast in the fall. He feels the large bunker moving down from the north bypass the South Jersey coast, while coming much closer to the coast in North Jersey. He claims the fall run of big fish is quite poor in South Jersey and this is the reason why. I never argue with the natives.

The one location along the Jersey coast where I know big stripers hang out in the fall is Shrewsbury Rocks. The bottom here is very rough, with many up and down ridges and valleys. All of this structure is to the striper's liking and they stay here as the bait moves through.

Trolling is the most popular technique here, with umbrella rigs a staple. Care must be taken to keep the rigs out of the structure by cranking up and letting out line as the contour changes.

The hill just off the old convention center in Asbury Park is another location where I have caught stripers. We marked them on the sonar and dropped jigs down to catch several school-size fish.

The fall striper run along the Jersey coast will begin in late September and run until after Thanksgiving, unless the weather turns cold and windy by early November. A warm fall could extend the action into December. There are many locations along the beach and out of the coastal ports where fall run stripers will be caught. Keep track of the migration through fishing reports in newspapers and magazines and be ready to go when the bite gets hot.

Delaware

The hot spot for fall fishing in Delaware is the mouth of Delaware Bay, either on the Cape May Rips or the Valley and the Eights close to the Lewes Breakwater. Hen and Chicken Shoal is another place where stripers are taken.

The number-one bait in the fall is a live eel. This is what just about all the charter and head boats use, and most of the private boats follow suit. In recent years, more private boats have started trolling with Mann's Stretch 25s, and I have had some luck pulling white bucktails across the bottom on wire line.

When I moved back to Delaware from Virginia Beach in 2000, I was anxious to try casting plugs to the Outer and Inner walls in the same fashion as I did to the rocks at the Chesapeake Bay Bridge Tunnel. Using a Wind-Cheater, I have worked both walls and have had some success. The best bite has been early in the morning on a flood tide that has just started out. I have found stripers and blues from the lighthouse on the Outer Wall to perhaps as far along the ocean side to the bend. Even so, most of the fish have come within 50 yards of the light.

On the Inner Wall, all of the stripers I have caught were under the light or in the rip that forms on the ebb tide. This wall does not produce as well as the Outer Wall, but I give it a shot every time I go out.

Fall surf fishing is best later in the season. I have heard stories from old timers about lubricating their Penn Squiders with kerosene and fishing the surf in late December. So far, I have not fished here that late, but have had some luck into November. Like all surf fishermen, we would love to see a striper blitz on the beach, but this is a rare occurrence in Delaware. Most of the time we soak a bunker head and wait for a bite. Over the years, Three Rs Road has been a good location for fall stripers.

Indian River Inlet has been alive with fall stripers for several years, but most fail to meet the 28-inch minimum size. Nevertheless,

boaters, rail birds and jetty jockeys crowd the inlet in hopes of finding that elusive keeper.

Harry Aiken is the master of fishing the inlet from a boat. He only uses a ¾-ounce hand-tied white bucktail dressed with a six-inch white worm. When we fish together I will use anything but a white bucktail and white worm, just to prove other lures will work. I must admit that on most, if not all, of our trips together he does catch more fish. Of course, he is much older than I, and my parents always said, "Don't embarrass your elders."

A green Tsunami shad worked slowly across the bottom works well at Indian River.

The lure I have the best success with at Indian River is a four-inch green Tsunami shad. I like to crawl it along the bottom as the boat drifts through the rip that runs from the green can to the entrance of South Shore Marina.

Fall striper fishing also includes the use of live spot, and many of the anglers at the inlet will fork over as much as two dollars each for this bait. Short stripers seem to appreciate the spot and eat them with abandon. The occasional keeper is taken on the live bait and I do believe spot are responsible for more large fish, but bucktails and shads put enough limits in my boat to keep me from feeding two dollar baits to the hoards of shorts.

White bucktails and white worms are the choice of the rail birds who line the sidewalk from the Southside Campground on the south side and from the Coast Guard Station on the north side, all the way out to the beach on the east side of the bridge. The same lure will also be found on the lines of jetty fishermen on both sides of the inlet.

I fish the rip that runs by the Coast Guard Station because there is a large parking area and porta-potties close by. Walking distances and proximity of facilities are serious considerations at my stage of life.

You need to make your best cast out past the rip so the current picks up the lure. Allow it to move out to the end of the rip, then work it slowly back so it crosses the current. Once it reaches the slower water, crank it back at a fair speed or it will sink to the bottom and stay there. I like a metal lure or green shad here, but most of my contemporaries use the white bucktail and worm combination. They rig it on a three-way swivel, with a one- to three-ounce sinker used to sink the bucktail to the strike zone. The technique is to let the rig bounce along the bottom until a fish hits or the sinker lodges between the rocks.

At night the live eel and black Bomber fishermen come out, and they find more keepers than the day shift. Other tempters after dark are black bucktails with black worms, black shads, and live sand fleas. The fleas are drifted without weight right in the rocks. In a strong current it may be necessary to add a small weight to get the bait below the surface. A circle hook tied directly to the 15- or 20-pound line is all you need.

Black tubes and twister tails make good eel imitations.

In November and December you can find large stripers feeding in the ocean under flocks of diving birds. When this happens, limits come quickly for trollers and casters alike.

Maryland Coast

Surf fishing in the fall along the Maryland coast is a matter of soaking bait and waiting for a bite. Stripers can be caught from the Delaware line all the way to Assateague on bunker, clams, and mullet.

The Route 50 Bridge in Ocean City holds good numbers of stripers in the fall, and anglers will take them during the night on live eels, Got-Cha plugs, and shads. The water under the bridge varies in depth from 10 feet or more to exposed sandbars. A trip at low tide during the day will reveal where the deeper water is located so you can find the drop-offs at night.

There is a pier on the southern tip of Ocean City, and it provides access to the top of the inlet. Live eels fished from here at night often provide keeper rockfish. There is a charge for fishing on the pier, and there is also a tackle shop with live bait.

The Ocean City Inlet is fished from shore at the north side and from boats from one end to the other. Live spot are the most productive bait during the day, with eels common after dark. As with Indian River Inlet, the boats can become congested, especially on the weekends.

Jetty fishermen use the usual white bucktails, shads, and plastic grubs. This is not a difficult jetty to fish, but caution should always be employed whenever you venture out on wet rocks.

Chesapeake Bay

Fall fishing in the Chesapeake Bay begins when the stripers school up and are found chasing bait on the surface. For the most part these will be small fish, but they are a ball to catch on light tackle or fly lines. This activity will begin in the upper bay during September and continue all the way down to the Chesapeake Bay Bridge Tunnel (CBBT) until the Virginia season closes on December 31.

Larger stripers will move into the bay from the coastal migration, and they can be distinguished by the presence of sea lice on the body. In the Maryland portion of the bay, trolling with big spoons, umbrella rigs, and plugs will be popular, as will chumming with bunker. The chance for a big striper here is not as good in the fall as it is in the spring, but because I have said that I expect the next Maryland state record to be caught here sometime in November.

The closer to the ocean you fish, the better your chance of connecting with a big striper. You will find boats from Point Lookout, Maryland, running below the Virginia line, and a number of Maryland charter boats spend the late season fishing out of Virginia Beach.

There will be flocks of birds diving on schools of feeding stripers from mid-October until the bay season in Virginia closes on December 31. Most of the time the stripers under these birds will be in the 18- to 24-inch range, but there will be occasions when larger fish to 40 inches will chase the same bait. The two different sized stripers do not travel together, so if you begin catching small fish, odds are that is all you will catch out of that school. One trick that I have found successful is to troll around the edge of the school with a large plug or spoon to catch a bigger class of fish.

When I ran charters here, some of my parties wanted to take home a limit and were not particular about the size. In that case, I would box the first limit we caught short one fish and would leave the slot open for a bigger striper if we happened to catch one. If not, we could fill the limit with another small fish.

Other parties were only interested in big fish. In that case, I would break out the wire line and join the crowd over the tunnel tubes.

The High Level Bridge at the north end of the CBBT is home to some really big stripers, and live eels are the way to get them out. Due to the depth of the water and the strong current here, wire line is used to get the eels down to the stripers.

There are numerous shoals and channels in the Virginia portion of the bay, and anglers will troll them moving south as the season progresses and the water cools. Boats out of Reedville, Deltaville, and Newport News catch plenty of big and small stripers on this structure.

Virginia Coast

A few anglers will go out to the barrier islands in the fall, and some will connect with big rockfish in the surf. Bait will be used more than lures, with fresh bunker leading the list.

The trailing parachute bucktail on a daisy chain caught this Virginia striper.

The author with a limit of Virginia stripers caught on the roll.

Trolling along the Virginia coast can be very productive. The current Virginia state record striper was caught out of Wachapreague in 2005. It was taken by Paul Kleckner and weighed 63 pounds, 8 ounces.

Trolling does not come into its own until after Thanksgiving, and in 2006 it was still going strong in February. The success and failure of the fall season is controlled by the weather. In 2005 we had a very mild October and November, but December was bitter cold. The stripers did not move down in any number before the cold spell, and when it was over, they were all the way down to North Carolina.

January was very warm and the stripers moved back north. By mid-January, they were thick right off the Virginia Beach coast and they were still being caught in great numbers in early February. What will happen in the future is anybody's guess.

Because the stripers will be big, most anglers pull Stretch 30s, Crippled Alewife spoons, umbrella rigs, or large Mojos. At times these lures will not be as effective as a one- or two-ounce bucktail or plastic shad if the stripers are feeding on small bait. Pay attention to the bait in the water and match your lure to the size of the local food.

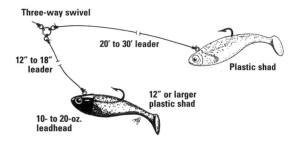

A Mojo rig.

There will be times when gannets and other birds dive on bait pushed to the surface by stripers. There will also be times when gannets dive on bait well below the surface, and stripers may or may not be in the area. Gannets swim deep and chase down their prey, so just because they are gathered in big flocks and hitting the water from dizzying heights, it may not mean the stripers are feeding under this activity. I have found stripers by trolling well away from the gannets along the edge of their activity when trolling closer did not produce.

Whales may also show up along the Virginia coast in late fall and early winter. They will attract much attention from the local seagull population, because whales are very sloppy eaters. Whatever the whales are dining upon will also be the special of the day for the stripers. Stripers have enough sense to keep away from the whales, which is more than I can say for some boaters, but they will be feeding somewhere in the general area.

North Carolina Coast

The end of the line for the fall migration is somewhere off the North Carolina coast. In cold years the fish will go as far as Hatteras Inlet, but more than likely they will stop somewhere between the Virginia line and Cape

Hatteras, and a few may show up on Ocracoke Island. At least this is as far as we catch them; they may go further south or east, but no one knows for certain.

This big North Carolina striper was jigged up near Duck.

Boaters have the upper hand here, as most stripers are taken by trolling or casting to large schools of fish. Here too, flocks of gannets and gulls are considered a good omen. A few very brave souls will work the shoals outside Oregon Inlet, but this is a dangerous undertaking.

Many of the boats fishing in North Carolina water come down from Virginia. They follow the stripers south and will travel as far as Oregon Inlet to find action.

In the surf, patience will be rewarded as anglers find big stripers on cut bunker. The stripers will be on the move, chasing schools of bunker and other bait, and may show anywhere along the North or South Beach. The point at Cape Hatteras is always a good bet, so long as you don't go past fish on the North Beach while driving down. In recent years Pea Island has held some good striper action, and, while it is closed to vehicles, the road is so close to the water it is possible to spot birds working in the surf while driving.

In January of 2006 there was a striper blitz in the surf near Corolla on the north end of the Outer Banks. The stripers were chasing bunker up on the beach, and everyone there had more 10- to 30-pound fish than they could count. Any lure that hit the water resulted in an immediate hook-up. Unfortunately, this only happened once that winter, and there were many days when the stripers were two very long casts from the beach.

The Herbert Bonner Bridge over Oregon Inlet will hold stripers, and anglers catch them from the catwalk on live spot or eels. A few are taken on darter plugs worked from the beach and cast to eddies around the pilings. This practice was brought to North Carolina by a bunch of New York Yankees—not the baseball team, just a group of Long Island fishermen. Both methods work much better after dark.

Roanoke River and Albemarle Sound

The Roanoke River runs from Virginia to the Albemarle Sound and is home to an interesting population of striped bass. The stripers spawn in the upper reaches of the river and then move down to the sound, with a few going so far as to join the coastal migration.

They attract anglers during the spring as they school up in the river, where light tackle and fly casters find exciting action. Much of this activity is centered around Roanoke Rapids in Halifax County, North Carolina.

Striper season is closed in the Albemarle Sound during the summer. It opens in the fall and lasts into the winter. The current limit is two per day, with a minimum size of 18 inches. Currituck and Croatan Sounds are also open during this season.

The primary areas where stripers are caught at this time of year will be around bridges and other hard structure. The Mann's Harbor Bridge that connects Roanoke Island with Dare County is a perfect example. Anglers gather here to cast bucktails to the pilings, either from the beach or from boats. At times, there will be 50-foot Carolina charter boats fishing here alongside small skiffs when the weather is too bad for the big boats to make it out of Oregon Inlet. Guides bring fly-fishing parties to the bridge, where they can catch a load of stripers.

During a fall trip to the area, I stopped by Pirate's Cove Marina on the east side of Roanoke Island to visit some friends. As I walked to the tackle shop I noticed one man fishing from the dock and catching stripers on every cast. My interest piqued as I watched him reach in a bait bucket, pull out a small croaker, hook it on the line, and toss it to the center of the harbor. In seconds a striper took the croaker and he had another fish on.

Upon closer inspection I saw a big school of small croaker literally trying to swim up a drainage ditch in a frantic effort to get away from the stripers in the harbor. They were packed in so tight all the angler had to do was dip them up with a net to keep his bait bucket stocked.

I ran back to my truck and rigged up a spinning rod with a bucktail. Upon returning to the dock I cast the lure to the same area my new friend was placing his croaker, but no matter what type of action I put on the bucktail I could not buy a strike. Before I left I tried plastic shads, Rat-L-Traps, WindCheaters, and several other lures, all to no avail. Those stripers wanted live croaker or nothing.

This entire area has spawned a new industry, as shallow water guides ply the sounds looking for stripers. They carry light tackle and fly fishermen to some very exciting action. You can also wade along the shores of the various sounds and cast with fly, jig, or plug. The beach behind Bodie Light is one popular spot, and you may also wade the flats adjacent to the Oregon Inlet Fishing Center.

Stripers Outside the Northeast
South Carolina

The major striped bass fishery in South Carolina is not along the coast, but in the freshwater impoundments of lakes Marion and Moultrie. These will be discussed in detail in the Freshwater chapter.

The river systems of South Carolina hold striped bass populations, but most are concentrated in the upper sections where the water is all but fresh. These stripers do not migrate along the coast in any numbers, and most of the fishing for them is concentrated in their native rivers.

Georgia

Here too, striper fishing is more popular in the freshwater impoundments than along the coast. Many of the stocks that were available in the lower portions of the rivers and bays have been significantly diminished by heavy industry and damming of rivers. Some rivers do hold fair numbers of stripers and most of the fishing for them is done further inland.

According to Chris Woodward, there are some stripers taken from the waters around Savannah, but not in numbers large enough to call it a fishery. There is no movement along the coast as these stripers keep themselves within the river systems.

Florida

I contacted some pretty well-versed anglers in Florida, and while they all knew about stripers in the St. Jones river system, none had actually caught any. Striper fishing is not very popular in the Sunshine State.

Gulf Coast

The Gulf Coast of Florida has an interesting population of striped bass. These fish never mix with the Atlantic stock and were all but extinct in the 1960s due to the destruction of their native habitat either by pollution or construction. The only remaining native stock was in the Apalachicola-Chattahoochee-Flint river system.

Today, due to conservation efforts by all the Gulf States, recreational fishermen are once again catching stripers. Once the massive cleanup was accomplished and the pollution controlled, millions of fry were stocked, and this has resulted in a good if not great fishery.

Alabama

The Tombigbee and Alabama rivers flow into Mobile Bay, and both rivers have a fishable population of stripers. The state record is a 55-pound cow caught in the Tallapoosa River, a tributary of the Alabama River. While stripers are found along the entire waterway of both the Alabama and Tombigbee rivers and their tributaries, they are seldom caught in the Mobile Bay estuary.

Mississippi

Here too, a massive restoration project is responsible for striped bass currently being caught in several rivers. The project has been successful to the point that recreational fishing tournaments are able to target stripers. Most of the stripers are found in the rivers, but the coastal fishery is improving.

Louisiana

The restoration work here has not gone as well as in Mississippi. In spite of large stockings of both fry and fingerlings, the coastal striper population is still not what one would hope. There is a large stock of stripers in Toledo Bend Reservoir, and the hatchery there has supplied the fry and fingerlings for the coastal program. Recreational anglers report a few stripers in the catch and a few more show up in commercial hoop nets.

Texas

In the 1800s, striped bass were the staple of commercial fishermen working the coastal bays of Aransas, Corpus Christi, and Galveston. Today, in spite of work by the Texas Parks and Wildlife Department, stripers are rarely caught in the state. The Department continues to stock hatchery fish and there are some signs of natural reproduction, but some time will pass before stripers become a staple of Texas recreational fishermen.

West Coast Stripers

The striped bass fishery on the West Coast owes its very existence to a trainload of Hudson River striper fry netted in the Navesink River that left New Jersey in 1879 and ended up in San Francisco Bay. By the time the train reached its final destination, only 132 stripers had survived the trip. These few fish, along with 300 more from the Shrewsbury River stocked three years later, expanded to form a good fishery in not only San Francisco but in Coos Bay, Oregon—where Joe Brooks caught his record fly-line striper in 1948—with some stragglers showing up as far north as British Columbia. Trolling seems to be the way most West Coast anglers bag their stripers, with some hardy souls fishing the rugged coastline from the beach. In years past the striper fishing was much better than it is today. The primary cause of the decline has been water diversion from the deltas where stripers had spawned. The water is used to irrigate crops, and there is simply not enough left to prevent saltwater intrusion. This in turn prevents the stripers from finding the almost-fresh water they need for a successful spawn.

Nine

Freshwater Stripers

There are two types of stripers found in fresh water. The first is a hybrid and the second is a true striper, just like the ones in salt water. The hybrid is a cross between a striper and a white bass, sometimes called a "wiper." They do not grow very large, but they do put up a good fight for their size. Most hybrids have broken lines along the body, and the body is a bit more rounded than a true striper. They have been stocked in numerous locations, but we will leave further discussion of hybrids to another time and another book and keep our focus on the true striped bass.

The true stripers found in fresh water began with migrating fish trapped behind a dam. In 1941 the federal government and the state of South Carolina were damming up the Santee and Cooper rivers to provide a hydroelectric generating station. When WWII was declared, the dams were complete but workers were still removing timber from the river bottoms. This was backbreaking, dangerous work in what was basically a Southern swamp. I have been told the men would bathe in kerosene before going to work in a vain attempt to keep the bugs off.

In the beginning of WWII, German subs were operating all along the Atlantic coast, and there was considerable concern they would land commandos who would damage such things as hydroelectric dams. The decision was made to close the gates of the dam in the spring of 1942 before the timber was removed. At the time no one considered the fact that stripers were on their spring spawning run up the Santee and Cooper rivers. When the dams were closed, the stripers were trapped, and they have been there ever since.

After the war men began to fish in the two new lakes created by the dams, and much to their surprise they caught stripers along with the more common largemouth bass, catfish, and perch. It did not take long before a thriving business community consisting of guides, lodges, tackle shops, and boat rentals sprang up in the Santee region.

The author with a Santee-Cooper striper.

As state biologists began to study these landlocked stripers, they discovered the fish behaved much the same way as their saltwater cousins. In the spring they traveled as far up the rivers as possible to spawn, then returned to the lakes. They also grew as large as the saltwater striper, with fish over 40 pounds caught.

Tiny Lund, a well-known stock car driver, ran a fishing camp and caught the state record striper, weighing 55 pounds. This record stood for 30 years. The current South Carolina state record striper is a 59-pound, 8-ounce fish from Lake Hartwell.

As word spread about the Santee-Cooper stripers, other states became interested in acquiring their own. Thus began the distribution of freshwater stripers across the country. Today these fish are available to anglers all across the United States.

Catching Freshwater Stripers

The same basic techniques used on saltwater stripers are used on freshwater stripers. My guess would be that most freshwater stripers are caught on live bait with various lures following behind. The live shad is the most popular bait because it is the top food source for stripers. In Santee-Cooper, the shad are suspended at various depths until stripers take notice. Most anglers set up a number of rods around the side of the boat in holders that keep them at a 180-degree angle to the water. The live shad is dropped on each line and the rods are left alone until a strike is detected, and the angler usually

Do not confuse this hybrid cross of a white bass and a striper with a freshwater striper.

waits until the rod tip touches the water before grabbing the rod to set the hook.

One interesting side effect of fishing live shad is that everything in the water will eat them. On one trip to the Santee-Cooper area, my friends and I caught a cooler full of blue catfish and not a single striper. The catfish were delicious. In some locations, anglers use live sunfish in place of shad, and I am sure other forage such as mill roach find their way into live wells.

Live shad make the top freshwater striper bait.

On another trip to Santee-Cooper, my group and I were fishing in the late afternoon and had a blitz of stripers on the surface and caught them one after another on bucktails. The next morning I was bait fishing for catfish with Al Ristori when the rockfish exploded all around the boat. My casting rod was still rigged with a bucktail from the night before, while Al had to dig a lure out of the paper bag he used as a tackle box and tie it on. I had a couple of stripers in the boat and Al was still working on his tackle. When I told him to look at all the stripers breaking around the boat, he replied that he was already nervous

enough and seeing all that activity would only make it harder to tie on the darn bucktail. He did accomplish the task in time to land a good number of nice rockfish.

The shad are set at various depths and the rods are placed in holders that keep them parallel to the water.

Today there are freshwater stripers in many states from California to Pennsylvania. A few of these stocks are able to sustain themselves with natural reproduction, while most require regular stocking. Several of the larger impoundments have such a good population of stripers that fishing tournaments are held there. The freshwater striper has also been stocked in many southern rivers to reestablish stocks wiped out by pollution and development.

I recently watched a show on TV where a well-known bass angler caught stripers from a Western impoundment on plastic shads. His target for the day was bass, but those darned old 10- to 15-pound stripers kept getting on the line. Don't you just hate it when that happens? It looked strange to see stripers caught from a body of water in the middle of the desert, where the surrounding landscape was completely devoid of vegetation.

Freshwater striper fishermen must learn the habits of their quarry just as their saltwater brethren. When do the fish feed? Do they come to the surface in the morning and afternoon? What do they eat? Is trolling, casting, or bait fishing most productive? Study the waters where you plan to fish and ask a lot of questions of the local striper anglers. As in salt water, it takes time to learn the ropes, but the reward is worth the effort.

A bass boat on an impoundment works well, though stripers weren't the bass such boats were named for.

Ten

A Few Words about Striper Boats

Because you'll catch stripers from a couple miles out in the ocean to shallow back bays, there is no perfect striper boat for every fishing situation. The 16-foot tin boat that works so well in sheltered, shallow water will be much too small for the ocean, and a deep-vee boat that can take the ocean waves will run aground in the shallows.

A deep-vee boat will run well in a head sea.

The one boat style that lends itself to all types of fishing is the center console. You can troll, cast, chunk, or drift from one of these versatile boats. There will be plenty of open deck space on most center console models, and even the smallest will have room for two or three anglers.

The drawback to a center console is the lack of protection from the weather. These are open boats with no cabin, and while you can rig one with enough canvas to shelter the occupants, this canvas defeats the purpose of an open boat, not to mention the difficulty of seeing through the windows when they are wet with salt spray. If a center console is your choice for a striper boat, I strongly suggest that you invest in a quality set of foul weather gear and plenty of warm clothes.

During most of my misspent youth I fished from center console boats, but as I aged the idea of being wet and cold lost some of its romantic charm. In 1992 I purchased a 24-Albemarle with a hardtop and full canvas. This is a heavy, deep-vee boat with a 24-degree dead rise carried to the stern. While it will roll around a bit when drifting in a beam sea, it will cut through a head sea when lesser boats are pounding their passengers to death. I have fished on just about every type of boat there is, and I like a deep-vee above all others.

A modified-vee hull is fine for inshore work.

Working a rip from the stern of a 24-Albemarle.

Just because I like a deep-vee hull with an enclosed cabin does not mean it is the right boat style for you. If you spend a lot of time drifting or anchored and chunking, you might find that the deep-vee tosses you around a bit too much. But if your friends and family go fishing with you on a regular basis, the lack of a head on a center console may be a problem.

The modified-vee bottom will handle a head sea reasonably well and is much more stable at rest than a deep-vee. A catamaran is very stable at rest and will take a head sea, but runs wet, as the spray developed between the hulls will blow back over the occupants when the boat is running into the wind.

I am seeing more Florida-style flats boats in use by striper fishermen. These fast little boats provide the maximum in open casting

room and will run in very shallow water. What they do not provide is a comfortable ride in any type of a sea, and with their low sides and flat bottom they will tend to be a bit wet. In Florida this is not a big problem, but it could be a serious problem in New England. So far, mostly fly fishermen bring the flats boats north because of the open space both forward and aft that lends itself to casting.

Long ago striper fishermen in New York and New England invented the bass boat. This is an open boat in the 20-foot class with an inboard motor and controls both forward and aft. Anglers used these boats to fish some very dangerous waters, from the rips at Sow and Pigs, the heavy surf off of Montauk, and the rocky shorelines found throughout the area. The captain has an excellent view of the water and his anglers from either the forward or aft controls. He can watch for submerged rocks at the aft controls and keep her headed in the right direction when working a rip from the forward controls. While some of the wooden classics still find use today, most of these boats currently on the water are made from fiberglass.

The one style of boat that I hate to see on anything but a small bass pond is the johnboat. The square bow, low sides, and flat bottom combine to make these boats very dangerous in open water. I have seen a johnboat sink from the wake of a passing sport fisherman.

The problems begin when a johnboat encounters even the smallest wave. The bow rises over the wave and the stern squats. The wave travels along the side until it reaches the stern, then it ships aboard. The added weight in the stern causes the boat to squat deeper into the water and the next wave has no trouble coming aboard. If that one does not sink the boat, the next one will. All of this takes a very few seconds.

For our discussion let's assume we have a 20- to 24-foot trailerable boat, either a center console or with a walk-around or cuddy cabin. This boat will be used in the open waters of the bays or ocean for everything from casting to trolling to chunking. Power can be outboard, inboard, or (I/O).

Once all the safety equipment is secured and stowed, the next problem is stowing the fishing equipment. Rods and reels present the biggest problem because you can't put them in a drawer, box, or similar container. I like to keep my rods in holders attached to the hardtop. This keeps them within easy reach yet out of the way. Most trailer boats have some sort of top, be it canvas or fiberglass, which will support six to eight holders. On striper trips my casting rods will be ready should we find a school of breaking fish. I will rig at least two and often three rods with different lures that I can easily switch off to if the original selection fails to produce.

My cabin has holders for six rods on the overhead, and this is where I stow my trolling rods. They are available, yet out of the way when I am casting. Because a trolling rig is a bit more involved than a casting rig, I keep them on leader spools and store the rods with just the ball-bearing snap swivel attached. I will pass the rods out from the cabin while a crewmember snaps on whatever trolling rig we are going to use. The opposite occurs when we pull the lines and head back home.

Most center console rigs have rod holders on the top as well as in front and alongside of the console. I would keep my casting rods on the top and the trolling rods in the front. The holders on the side should never be used to store rods that have rigs or lures attached. The space between these rods and the side of the boat is quite narrow and some fishermen, including myself, are not. A wide fishermen passing through a narrow area lined with hooks is a recipe for disaster.

While striper boats do not need outriggers, they do need outroders. These devices hold the rod almost at a 90-degree angle to the water and put more distance between the lines when trolling. They are a necessity when wire line trolling with bunker spoons and a big help in all trolling situations. They fit into the rod holders along the gunwale.

Outroders are a good idea on a striper boat.

Electronics on a striper boat would be the same as any other boat. You must have a VHF radio (not a cell phone or portable VHF), a sonar, and a GPS. Radar is very handy when bad weather moves in, especially fog. It is not absolutely necessary but it does add a level of confidence. Radar will also keep you within the three-mile limit, or at least let you know when you cross the line.

The newer GPS models have a chart built in, and this too is a good way to keep track of where you are. Just remember if you are caught outside the three-mile limit, the only equipment that counts is on the Coast Guard or local law enforcement boat. These charts combined with the sonar unit will help you track on a channel edge, anchor at the top of a slough, or keep going back to the same location where the stripers are holding.

While electronics are great, they sometimes fail, leaving you to navigate on your own. For this reason I strongly recommend taking a navigation course and buying a good compass and set of charts. True, striper fishermen seldom lose sight of land, but when the GPS and radar fail in the fog, you'll do well to have some idea of how to find the inlet. This is why I always keep track of my course home should I need a heading and the GPS decides to die. Once I have arrived at my chosen fishing spot I bring up the waypoint for the run back and keep it on for the rest of the trip, unless I pick up and move to a new location. After arriving at the new spot, the GPS goes back to the home waypoint.

Even the most expensive electronics in the world won't catch a fish. The angler must learn to operate his equipment correctly and use the information it provides to find where the fish are holding. Begin by reading the operation

manual several times before ever leaving the dock. Once on the water, practice with the gear until it becomes familiar. Determine what a certain color or shape on the sonar means. Is it bait, stripers, bluefish, or croaker? Is the bottom rock, mud, or sand? Are you on the edge of the channel or off too far in the deep? All of this takes experience, and once you can interpret the information you are well on your way to catching more and bigger stripers. By the way, don't start practicing in the middle of a striper blitz. Get on the water when the action is not too good so the fish won't distract you.

Tackle storage is always a problem even on the biggest boats. There is a law of the sea that states no matter how much room there is for tackle on a boat, the owner will fill it with lots of stuff and have even more stuff left over.

Tackle storage is made easier with plastic storage trays.

My Albemarle came with three small tackle drawers that hold next to nothing. To solve my tackle problems, I used a bunch of those small tackle boxes with a different type of lure or whatever in each one. I have two Plano boxes that hold three of these smaller boxes and I keep my most used tackle in them. I store the other small tackle boxes in two larger plastic containers along with my flares, emergency water and food, line, leaders, hooks, and sinkers. These containers are stored on the vee berth in the cabin.

Many of the newer boats have a bit more tackle storage, but it is never enough. The larger center console boats have a lot of open space in the console where tackle may be stored. Many have a head in there as well. Each boat is different, and each angler will have his favorite way to store his tackle. Just be sure it is all out of the way when the boat is running or fishing.

Make sure all the tackle and electronics are portable. I never leave anything on my boat when not in use. To do so only invites thieves, even if the boat is in your yard. I did leave some fishing stuff on my Albemarle when it was in dry storage. The boat was stored about 20 feet in the air in a locked building so I felt somewhat secure. Even then I still removed all of my electronics.

The one item that every boat needs is a five-gallon bucket. It will find use as a trash can, live well, lure holder, bait container, and a thousand other things. Never leave the dock without one.

Small boats that are used in sheltered, shallow water have even less storage space. My 16-foot Starcraft is completely open except for a small bin under the forward deck that carries the batteries for my electric trolling motor. There is another very small storage area on the port side that I use to keep my safety equipment and charts.

I purchased a canvas bag that holds four of the small plastic tackle boxes inside and two very small boxes on the side. It is easy to carry, stows under one of the seats, and holds all the tackle I need. I can switch out the boxes when I change from stripers to flounder or whatever is in season.

Homemade rod holders on the author's 16-foot tin boat.

The ever-useful five-gallon bucket holds trolling lures ready for work.

My rods are stored in five holders the previous owner installed along the port side. This is fine when running, but the rods will get in the way when casting. I take them out of the holders and lay them on top of the small bin and live well, where they will be safe and out of my way. I place them back in the holders when returning to the dock to prevent me from stepping on them while trying to get out of the boat.

The stern carries two rod holders that I can use while trolling or drifting. They are made of hard plastic and will hold spinning or conventional outfits. The console in the tin

Even a small boat can carry a selection of helpful electronics.

boat holds a compass, sonar, and a portable GPS. A VHF radio is under the console and the antenna is clipped to the gunwale until I need it. I do not keep the radio on all day; I just use it in emergency situations.

The anchor and line are stored in an open compartment under the forward deck. I like to have it handy in case of an emergency.

The electric trolling motor is secured to the bow, and the foot control reaches back to the console. I can operate it while standing or sitting. The seat that was on the bow has been moved to the stern. I find my fly casting friends

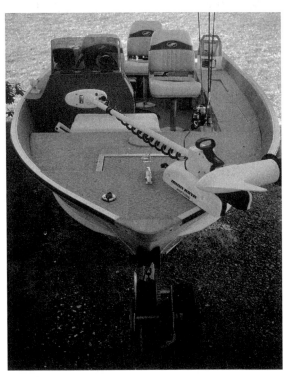

A trolling motor makes shallow water fishing much easier.

would rather have the bow open than try to cast around the seat. As for me, I am way too clumsy to stand or even sit on the bow.

The two gas tanks, one 10-gallon and one 3-gallon, with separate fuel lines are stowed under the splash well along with the starting battery.

I can use the Starcraft to fish the back bays, inside the inlets, and in the Delaware Bay

This is about as far as you can take an inflatable raft, on a calm day.

close to shore when weather conditions permit. Even in the best sea conditions you can expect some spray when running in a beam sea, so foul weather gear is the uniform of the day.

Boat Handling

Striper fishing is often good when the weather is bad. The captain has sole responsibility as to when the boat will go, but every fisherman on board has the responsibility to take care of himself. Even if the captain says he is going, you can say it is too rough or dangerous for you to join him. I know you will hear some chiding from your friends, but you have to get over it. No fish is worth dying for and few are worth taking a beating and being scared half out of your mind.

That said, you can fish in some pretty sloppy conditions if you know how to handle your boat. The first thing to do when the seas build is slow down. If the hull is pounding, you are going too fast.

Fishing a shoal or reef in the ocean is very dangerous. The seas will build over the shallow water and break right in your boat if you do not approach the area correctly. I troll a shoal by running along the inshore side, keeping my

distance from the breaking waves. It is possible to work the offshore side, but most of the time the stripers will be lying in the white water waiting for a bait to move past. You need good judgment and experience to run the boat close enough to the white water to put the lures in the strike zone without putting the boat in danger.

You can cast to the white water below a shoal, and casting may be the preferred technique in locations where making a safe trolling pass is not possible. The captain must hold the boat in position so the angler can reach productive water. He may stay in one general location or move slowly along the shoal as the angler works the entire area.

The waves on any given shoal will break differently depending on the direction of the wind and current. This means they will break differently as the tide cycles from high to low and back again, even if the wind maintains its original direction.

When the wind is onshore, the waves will build as they move to the beach. When they encounter the shoal, they will break from considerable height and with considerable force. This is a very dangerous situation for any boat and many captains avoid working this type of water. Those that do give the waves a great deal of respect because they know there is no forgiveness in this situation.

An offshore wind will hold down the wave height close to shore, but large waves born in the ocean will still crash on the shoal. Working the inshore side of the shoal will be a little safer, as the wind will blow off the tops of the waves. Still, it is a dangerous situation.

Some of the worst shoals are found off the mouth of Oregon Inlet in North Carolina.

Local charter captains seldom have problems, while more than one out-of-area crew has been lost in these treacherous waters.

Rips can also prove challenging. Here the current running over a drop, hill, ridge, or other bottom structure will build standing waves. When the wind and the current are in sync, the waves will not be too bad; however, when they oppose each other things will become interesting.

In either case, approach the waves from the upcurrent side so your lures or bait will be carried back to the fish waiting below the rip. Troll very slowly parallel to the rip, with the bow of the boat pointed into the current. Maintain just enough speed to keep the boat from moving back into the rip.

Drifting through the rip can really be exciting. Begin upcurrent and try to keep the boat heading with the direction of the current flow. Be ready to power up if the boat begins to slide backward, where it can be swamped by the breaking waves. Don't give the boat too much power or it may go over the waves and pitchpole.

When the boat reaches the downcurrent end of the rip, you'll have to run back to the upcurrent end and begin the drift again. *Do not* run the boat back across the rip. Run way around and off to the side as far away from the fish as possible. By staying away from the center of the rip, you not only keep from spooking the fish, but you also don't create a wake that will only add to the difficulty of fellow fishermen who are trying to maintain their drift through the rip.

All of this is difficult enough in the daytime; at night it is much more of a challenge. The best teacher is experience, and going out several times with an experienced captain is a good way to start.

Trolling or drifting in open water is not as difficult as it is on shoals or rips. I have a personal rule that seas over three feet or wind over 20 knots will keep me at the dock. There have been a few times when the marine weather forecast was wrong, and I found myself in bigger seas than expected. This can happen when the wind and current are opposed or an offshore low has caused large seas. It also happens when the dunderheads at NOAA don't have enough sense to stick their heads out of a window to see what is really going on outside. But I digress.

A trailer boat rigged for striper fishing.

When trolling in rough conditions, either head into or with the seas. Running in a beam sea is not only uncomfortable, but somewhat dangerous. A beam sea can break over the side of the boat and cause it to sink.

Keep in mind when heading into the current the speed of the water along the hull and over the lures will increase. The opposite occurs when running with the current. The engine speed will need adjusting to maintain proper lure action. Normally, it is a very small adjustment, just a few RPM, but trolling a lure too fast or too slow can be the difference between catching stripers or hauling water.

If you have a sum log speed indicator it will tell you how fast the water is moving past the boat and lure. The GPS gives you the boat's speed over the bottom. Before putting the lures back in the spread, run them alongside the boat and adjust the engine speed until the lure has the proper action. At this point check the sum log and make a note of the speed. As the direction and the strength of the current changes, you can keep the lure running correctly by maintaining the same speed on the sum log.

Some lures have a distinctive vibration that is transferred to the rod tip. Once you have some hours on the water trolling with these lures, you will notice when the rod is vibrating properly, when weeds foul the line, and when the lure goes too fast or too slow.

Boat handling comes with experience. The captain will become one with his boat and make little corrections without thinking about why. He must be aware of what is going on around him at all times and always remember he is responsible for the crew and all actions he makes.

Eleven

Knots

No one can be a successful fisherman unless he or she can tie good, strong knots. The connection between fish and angler is only as strong as the weakest knot, and all of those stories about a how big the fish that got away must have been because it snapped 50-pound line are more than likely the result of a bad knot.

Always begin tying any knot with plenty of line. When you use monofilament, always wet the line before pulling the knot tight. Dry mono will not seat properly and the knot will be weak. Most anglers put the line in their mouth and wet it with spit.

There must be hundreds of knots used by fishermen all over the world, but for our purpose I will illustrate those most useful for striper fishing. We will not get into knots for fly fishing because that would be an entire other book.

Improved Clinch Knot

This is a knot I have been using ever since I first learned to tie knots. I use it to attach just about everything to monofilament line, and,

when tied correctly, it will not fail. I use five or six wraps with line testing less than 15 pounds and three wraps when using line up to 50-pound test. This is an easy knot to learn and can be tied in the dark, a very important benefit for striper fishermen who often fish at night.

1. Thread the tag end of the line through the eye of the hook or lure and pull five to six inches of line alongside the standing part. Make four to five wraps around the standing line, then put the tag end back through the loop between the first wrap and the eye of the hook or lure. Now bring the tag end back through the loop between the wraps and the standing line.

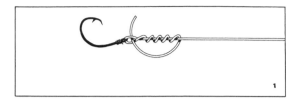

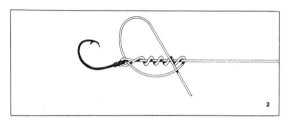

2. Wet the line and pull the knot tight with a slow, steady pressure. Finally, tighten the knot by pulling on the hook or lure with pliers while pulling on the line with your hands.

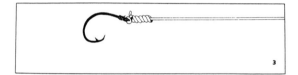

Snelling a Hook

When using a hook with a turned up or down eye, it is best to snell it to the leader. By doing so, the line will be pulling directly on the shaft of the hook, which should help with setting the hook and keeping it in place. While this knot may be tied on site, it is much better to snell all of your hooks before leaving home.

1. Pull at least 12 inches of line through the eye of the hook, then put the tag end back through the eye once more to form a loop.

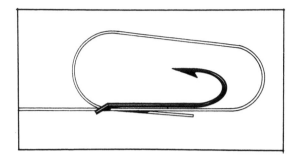

2. Wrap the loop around the shank of the hook six times. It requires a bit of manual dexterity to keep pressure on the wraps so they do not unwind as you go.

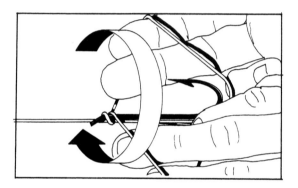

3. Keep pressure on the wraps while pulling on the standing line until the remainder of the loop is under the wraps. Slide the knot towards the eye until it is snug against it. At this point, pull on the tag end with pliers while pulling on the standing line with your other hand to make sure the knot is tight.

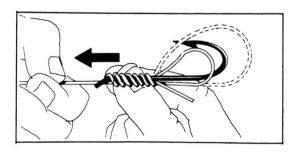

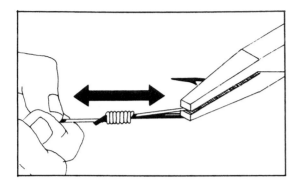

Simple Blood Knot

This knot may be used when joining two lines when the diameter of one is no greater than twice the diameter of the other. I use it to join a light monofilament line to a shock leader.

1. Lay the two lines next to each other with a six- to eight-inch overlap, and pinch them between your finger where the tag ends cross. Begin by wrapping the lighter line (the darker line) seven times around the heavier line (coming from the right).

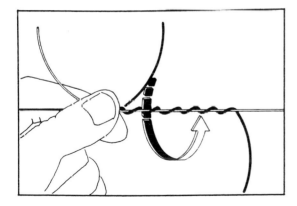

2. Next, cross the tag ends, pinch them between your thumb and finger, and wrap the heavy line tag end around the lighter standing line

seven times, from left to right. Pull the tag ends through this loop.

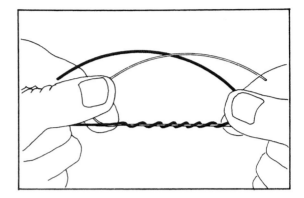

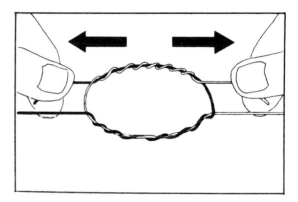

3. Begin to tighten the knot by pulling on both tag ends. Alternate between pulling on the tag ends and the standing line as you slowly tighten the knot.

4. When the knot is properly tied, the two tag ends will be opposed to each other, and the coils will stack up evenly, forming a solid barrel shape. Give a final pull on the standing lines, then trim the tag ends as close as possible to the knot. Be careful when trimming the tag ends so you don't nick the knot, as this will cause premature failure. Don't ask how I know.

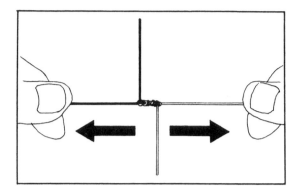

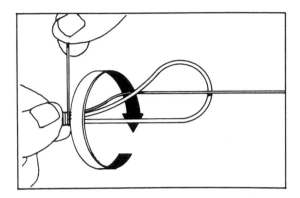

Albright Knot with a Lock

I use this knot to join my braided running line to a monofilament leader. I never fish with braided line tied directly to the lure or snap, so this knot is found on most of my outfits.

1. Begin by forming a loop in the thicker line, usually the monofilament.

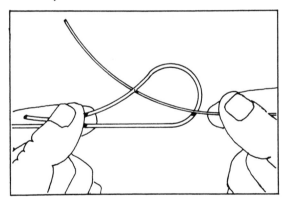

2. Bring the tag end of the thinner line, usually the braid, through the loop and, using your thumb, hold it tight to the thicker line beyond the end of the loop. Wrap the thinner line around the base of the loop of thick line (around both strands). Use at least twelve wraps, making each one tight to the previous wrap.

3. When the wraps are complete, pull the tag end of the thinner line back through the thicker loop from the same direction from which it entered.

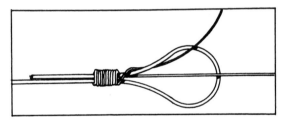

4. Work the wraps towards the end of the loop with your thumb while pulling on the tag and the standing part of the thinner line simultaneously. When the wraps can go no farther and are seated against the thicker line (the loop has been pulled closed), pull the tag end tight with a pair of pliers.

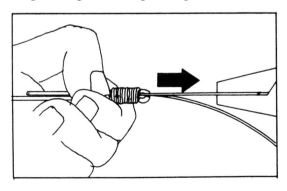

5. To finish the knot, pull both standing lines to completely seat the knot.

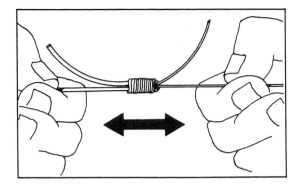

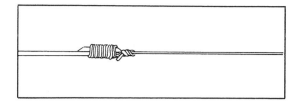

Nonslip Loop

Use this knot on jigs, plugs, and spoons when you want the lure to have some freedom to move around. Be sure to make the proper number of turns with the tag end, depending on the size of the line. Up to 6-pound test, use seven turns. For lines between 8- and 12-pound test, use five turns. Use four turns for 15- to 40-pound test, three turns for 50- to 60-pound line, and two turns for any leader heavier than 60-pound test.

6. To lock the knot, loop the tag end of the thinner line three times around itself and back towards the thicker line.

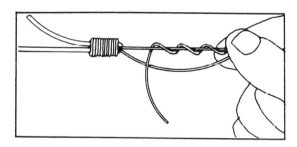

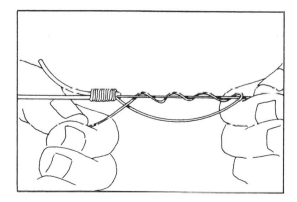

1. Make an overhand knot in the standing line, creating a loop, and pass the tag end through the eye of the hook or the lure. Pull about 12 to 13 inches of the tag-end line back through the loop on the same side from which it exited.

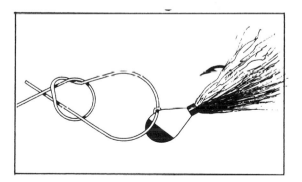

7. Secure the wrap by pulling on the tag end until the thinner line is tight against the knot.

2. Make two to seven wraps around the standing line with the tag end.

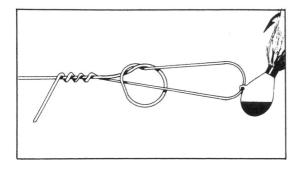

3. Put the tag end back through the loop, once again making sure it goes through from the same side it first exited towards the lure.

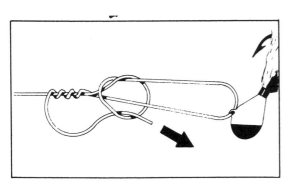

4. Pull the tag end to tighten the wraps around the standing line. Now, with the lure or hook in one hand and the standing line in the other, pull the loop knot tight.

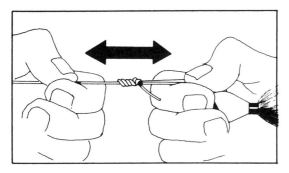

Perfection Loop

This is the knot to use on the end of leaders tied to either hooks or lures. Once you have this knot mastered, it can be tied very quickly in daylight or dark.

1. Hold the line between your thumb and forefinger about six or seven inches from the tag end and form a loop, with the tag end going under the standing line.

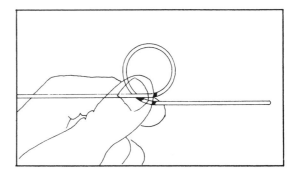

2. Create a second loop in front of the first and hold both together between the thumb and forefinger.

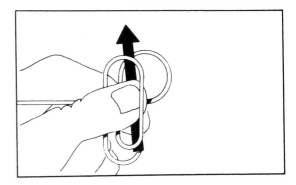

3. Lay the tag end between the two loops, then pull the second loop through the first loop.

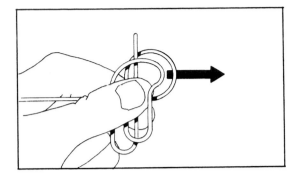

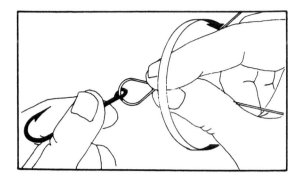

4. Keep pulling on the second loop while keeping the knot together by holding it between the thumb and forefinger. I use a pair of pliers to finish the knot by putting the pliers through the loop while pulling on the standing line.

2. Here is the most important part: Twist the wires together at the same time, keeping them at the 90-degree angle. Use three to four Haywire wraps and the loop should appear as in the illustration. Notice how the two lines are twisted together, not one over the other.

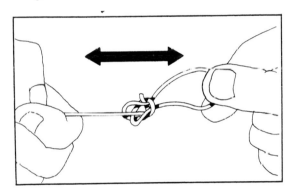

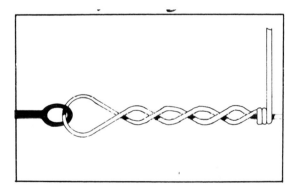

Haywire Twist

This knot is employed for many purposes, but striper fishermen use it primarily to join single strand wire line to the Dacron backing or to the snap swivel that connects the wire line to the leader.

1. Either form a loop or pull the tag end of the wire through the swivel. Place the tag end at a 90-degree angle over the standing part of the wire.

3. Finish the loop with a barrel wrap by wrapping the tag end around the standing part. Bend the tag end so you can grab it and break it off right at the end of the barrel wrap.

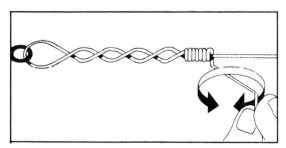

4. Breaking the tag end off as opposed to cutting it off with pliers leaves the wire smooth, with no danger of cutting anyone who may come in contact.

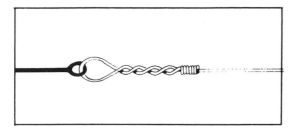

Figure Eight Knot

I use this knot to join braided wire line to the snap or three-way swivel on the tag end.

1. Pass three to five inches of the braided wire through the swivel or snap. Put the tag end under the standing part to form a loop.

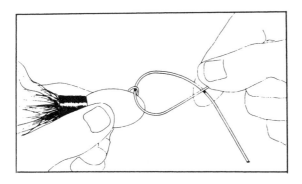

2. Form the figure eight by putting the tag end over the standing part. Pull the tag end back through the first loop.

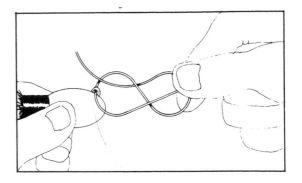

3. To tighten the knot, pull on the tag end with a pair of pliers.

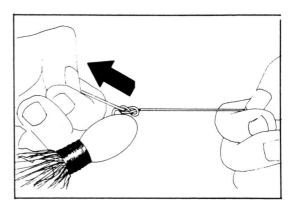

4. Do not pull on the standing part to tighten a figure eight knot. This will crimp the wire, as shown in the top drawing. The finished knot should look like the bottom drawing, with the standing part running straight off the knot.

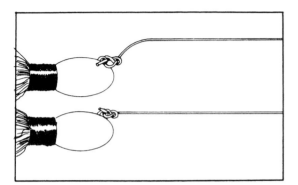

Practice all of these knots until you can tie them quickly and efficiently. Be sure to check each knot after it is tied to make sure it looks right, and then pull on it using pliers or gloves to make sure it will not slip.

Twelve

Catch-and-Release, Cleaning and Cooking

Catch-and-release is a critical part of striper fishing, if for no other reason than the great number of stripers available and the very low bag and high size limits. An angler can catch a two-fish bag limit in a matter of minutes when the action is hot, and no one wants to stop catching just because the bag is full. The other situation is a sea full of stripers, and none big enough to keep. In this case many anglers will break out the light tackle and keep right on catching. Should a nice-size keeper show up, the angler would find out just how good a fisherman he is.

In my opinion, the key to safe catch-and-release fishing is barbless hooks on lures and circle hooks with bait combined with tackle strong enough to land the fish quickly. Catch-and-release is no place for light tackle that will wear the fish down and make it too tired to recover. When I ran charters, I would have the party use barbed hooks until they had a limit in the box, then I would switch out the lures to ones with barbless hooks. We were fishing in the lower Chesapeake with an 18-inch size limit, and the number of stripers we caught below that limit I could count on one hand.

When fishing in an area like Indian River Inlet, where most of the stripers will be below the 28-inch limit, barbless hooks should be used all the time. The same holds true for trolling when in an area where you are likely to connect with a short.

Making a hook barbless is easy. Simply crush the barb with a pair of fishing pliers. Be careful when crushing barbs on treble hooks as

147

a slip can impale one of the unmodified barbs into a sensitive part of the anatomy.

Barbless hooks will hold a fish as well as a hook with a barb if the angler keeps a tight line. Give the fish slack line and there is a good chance the hook will fall out for a long-line release. The main reason I like barbless hooks is because I do not have to remove the striper from the water in order to remove the hook. An added benefit is that should a stray hook find its way into someone's hide, it is much easier to remove than if it were buried beyond the barb.

Return a fish to the water by slowly moving him in the current until his strength returns.

When possible grab the lure and remove the hook without moving the fish out of the water.

Most of the time, all I have to do is grab the lure with the fish still in the water and slide the hook out. When using a plug with two or more sets of treble hooks, it is possible for the striper to be hooked in more than one location. In this case it may be easier to bring the fish into the boat before removing the hooks. Even then you are way ahead of the game because the hooks will come out so much easier with less stress on you and the fish. Should the striper be big enough to net, the hooks will also come out of the net with relative ease.

Speaking of nets, the new plastic-coated nets are supposed to help preserve the slime coating on the striper better than the old twine nets. This slime is a protective coating that keeps the striper from contracting bacterial infections. To further protect this slime coat, handle the fish with a towel or rag that has been soaked in seawater.

There will be times when releasing a striper while it is still in the water is impossible. Head boats, where the height of the boat keeps the fish too far away, and fishing from bridges or jetties are examples of this situation. In most cases, you should be able to swing small fish to you by cranking out the slack while pointing the rod tip towards the fish, then swinging it aboard. Rock jetties pose a bit of a problem because most of the time you are not directly above the fish. If possible, walk down to the water and lift the fish out. If not, do the best you can by lifting the fish over the rocks, and don't drag it ashore. A long-handle net may help in this situation. A gaff should never be used when there is any possibility that the fish will be released. It is far better to lose a 29-inch striper than to kill a 27-incher because you thought it might be a keeper.

Another thing to avoid is putting your hands anywhere near the gills of a fish you plan to release. Hold the fish by the lower jaw, much like those TV bass fishermen (kissing is optional), or cradle it, supporting the head and body. Release the fish headfirst. In the case of a big striper that may be tired after the fight, move it back and forth in the water to push water over its gills until it regains some strength. I usually do this by holding the lower jaw. If the boat is moving slowly forward it will not be necessary to move the fish yourself. Big stripers indicate they are ready for release by clamping down on your thumb.

There have been occasions when I have seen anglers toss fish back by throwing them through the air to land on their side, back, or head. This is not only bad for the fish, it makes the angler look like an idiot. I don't care if the striper was too small to keep; there is no excuse for mistreating the animal. A short flight with a crash landing may stun the fish, slowing its recovery from the fight and making it vulnerable to predators. With all the so-called animal rights groups trying to stop catch-and-release and fishing in general, all they need is some home video of a half-drunk nut job throwing stripers around like a Frisbee to raise a stink, and raise money.

One occasional aspect of catch-and-release fishing is the necessity to throw back a striper that is going to die. I know it seems like a waste, but it must be done. If you have a limit already or the fish is too short, no matter how seriously the fish is injured, it must go back. You don't want to risk the penalty if you're caught over the bag limit.

The fishery managers who regulate stripers count on an 8 percent mortality rate for catch-and-release fishing when the water temperature is cool. That figure jumps to 90 percent in fresh water when the water temperature reaches above 70 degrees. Fortunately, saltwater catch-and-release is not as adversely affected by warm water as fresh, but it is still a good idea to restrict your catch-and-release fishing to cooler weather.

As I noted in an earlier chapter, live-bait fishing in warm water is deadly, in my personal experience. I have no scientific study to confirm this fact, but in talking with biologists familiar with striped bass they have given a few reasons why this is so. Stripers tend to take live bait deeper than lures thereby adding to the mortality from deep-hooked fish. Another factor is the warm water that puts additional strain on the fish somewhat like the difference between doing hard work in cooler weather, and doing hard work in 70 percent humidity.

There were a few charter and private vessels catching stripers on live croaker or trout over the tunnel tubes at the Chesapeake Bay Bridge Tunnel after the Virginia striper season closed on June 15. I had been fishing downcurrent from them and constantly saw dead stripers floating past. In order to verify what was going on, Claude Bain, Director of the Virginia Saltwater Fishing Tournament, and I went out and fished the tube with live bait. We only caught three stripers before we stopped because none of the three could be revived. I realize this is not a valid study, but it sure convinced us that live-bait catch-and-release fishing, especially in warm water, was a bad idea.

Bait fishing is by its nature more likely to result in injury to the fish than fishing with artificials. Bait is a natural tasting food to the striper and he is less likely to spit it back out than a strange tasting lure. This problem intensifies when live bait is used, because the striper must swallow it headfirst and that puts the hook in close proximity to the gills and stomach.

Circle hooks will solve most of these problems, and even when they do come in contact with internal organs, it is usually the gill rakers. With a little luck and some delicate work with a pair of pliers, the hook can be removed without damage to the gills.

There is some conflict about what to do when a hook cannot be removed. One school of thought says cut the leader as close as possible to the hook, while another feels it is better to leave the leader attached because it will help the fish dislodge the hook. I go with cutting the leader close to the hook, but the choice is as much personal as scientific. In either case, the hook will eventually rust out or fall out if the striper does not die first from the injury. The use of stainless steel hooks is not recommended because they take much longer to deteriorate.

I have been using circle hooks for all of my bait fishing for the past 10 years, and to date I have not encountered any problems that were not my own fault. When I first made the switch from J hooks to circle hooks, I would try to set the hook and usually ended up missing the fish. The trick with circle hooks is to do as little as possible and let the hook do all the work.

When a pickup or bite is detected, let the line come tight and simply crank in the fish. If there is slack in the line, crank it out while keeping the rod tip pointed to where the line enters the water. The circle hook travels along the inside of the mouth until it reaches the corner, where it turns and the point penetrates the skin. Not only is this a safe place to hook the fish, it is also a very good location for the hook to set. You normally will not have to worry about this hook falling out or cutting through the skin because the curve of the hook will settle in the corner of the mouth at the latch. This does make it a bit of a job to remove, but if you just back it out the way it went in, all will be fine.

Some jurisdictions have made the use of circle hooks mandatory when bait fishing for stripers. Others are looking at the idea.

Catch-and-release fishing for stripers has become a way of life and is one of the reasons the sport has become so popular. Anglers have a responsibility to practice catch-and-release in the safest manner possible to ensure the survival of the fish and the continuation of this sport.

Clean and Cook

While catch-and-release is a lot of fun, cleaning and cooking striped bass has its rewards. Striped bass have been a part of my diet ever since I can remember, with the exception of the moratorium when possession of stripers was prohibited.

The most important thing to do when keeping stripers for the table is put the fish on ice as soon as it is caught. I don't care if the weather is freezing, put the striper on ice in a cooler and add some seawater to make a bit of a brine. This water will keep the fish moist and chill it even quicker than ice alone. Not only is a cold fish going to stay fresher, it will be much easier to clean than a fish that has been allowed to dry out on deck.

Clean the fish as soon as possible when you get back to the dock. I know sometimes it is late at night and everybody is tired, but a few minutes spent at the cleaning table before heading home will make for a better meal. If you do not know how to clean a striper, have a professional fish cleaner do the job. I'll give you cleaning instructions in this chapter, but some people prefer to have someone else do the dirty work. I have someone clean my fish when I know the trash man won't be picking up for several days. Something about week-old fish guts in the trash adds a certain fragrance to the air, making me very popular with the local cats and very unpopular with the neighbors.

The following photos show how to fillet a striper with a fillet knife. You can also scale the fish, cut off the head, tail and fins, and take out the guts. This will give you the striper body that some folks like to cook whole or stuff. I have found it just as convenient to use fillets for all my striper dishes, and the fillets store much easier in the freezer.

Run the blade down the back making a one-inch deep cut.

Cut down to the backbone as you pull the meat away from the ribs.

At the end of the stomach cavity cut away the meat on both sides of the backbone.

When filleting a striper begin the cut behind the head.

Sever the meat from the ribs around the stomach cavity and cut the skin down to the tail. Leave the skin attached to the tail fin.

Hold the fillet of the fish while running the knife blade between the skin and the meat.

Continue to run the blade all the way to the end and the meat will separate from the skin.

The end result, a perfect, skinless fillet.

When using an electric filet knife make the first cut behind the head.

Then, without removing the knife, continue cutting along the backbone and through the ribs around the stomach cavity. Do not cut the meat away from the tail.

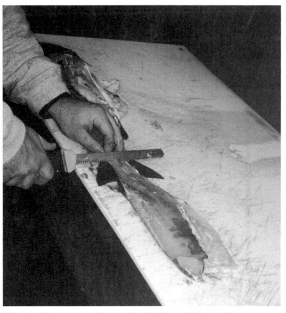

Flip the filet over and run the knife under the skin.

Cut the skin away from the entire filet including the meat at the stomach.

The filet is separated from the skin, but the ribs around the stomach are still attached.

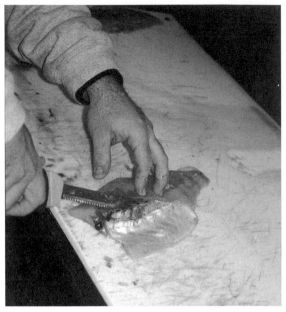

Use the knife to cut away the ribs by cutting between the end of the ribs and the body.

Continue to cut the entire rib section away.

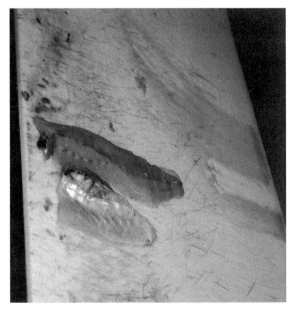

Once again the finished product is a boneless and skinless filet.

Recipes

There are thousands of cookbooks out there with millions of recipes for cooking fish. And any recipe that calls for a mild, white meat fish will work with striped bass.

I like my stripers with as little added flavor as possible. I will either fry them up and serve with French fries and coleslaw, or bake them in butter with a bit of lemon juice.

I do not like these new restaurants that serve a little pile of something I cannot identify in the middle of a big plate with some sort of stuff dribbled all over everything. If I am eating off of a big plate, I want it covered with food from one side to the other and I want to be able to tell what I am eating. The following recipes will fill the plate and the diner with good food and you will know what you are eating.

Frying

4 to 6 striper fillets
2 eggs
1 cup bread crumbs
Salt and pepper to taste

Beat the eggs in a shallow bowl. Dip fillets in egg mixture. Coat with bread crumbs. Drop into hot fat or cooking oil. Fry about two to four minutes per side, depending on thickness. Drain on paper towels. I like to use malt vinegar on the fish and French fries. Baked beans go well with this. Wash down with a big glass of iced tea.

Baking

4 to 6 striper fillets
Butter or margarine
Juice from 1 lemon

Place fillets in glass baking pan. Cover with butter or margarine. Drizzle lemon juice over fish. Cover with aluminum foil and bake 20 to 30 minutes, depending on thickness, in a 350-degree oven.

Stuffed Rockfish

This is a favorite dish along the Eastern Shore of Maryland and Virginia, where it is normally made with a whole rockfish. I use rockfish fillets, and to date no one has complained.

6 to 8 striper fillets
1 pound crabmeat
1 tablespoon bread crumbs
3 tablespoons mayonnaise
2 teaspoons Worcestershire sauce
1 egg
Old Bay seasoning to taste

Beat the egg in a bowl, then add all other ingredients and mix completely. Lay four to six fillets on the bottom of a glass baking dish that has been sprayed with oil. Add crab mix to cover fillets. Lay four to six fillets on top of crab mix. Sprinkle with more Old Bay. Bake in a 350-degree oven for 30 to 40 minutes. Test the fish for doneness after 30 minutes. The meat should flake easily.

Grilled Striper

To grill a striper or any other fish, use one of those fish baskets or a small grill that goes over the larger one and has very small grates. If not, the fish may stick to or fall through the normal grates on a grill.

4 to 6 striper fillets
Old Bay seasoning to taste
Butter, margarine, or olive oil

Melt butter or margarine and brush on fillets. If using olive oil, just brush it on. Shake on Old Bay. Put fillets in fish basket or on small grill over low heat. Keep an eye on what you are doing because the oil or butter will cause the flames to jump up, and if you are not careful you can burn the meat. It will only take a few minutes to cook the fish, so keep turning it so it will cook evenly.

To Eat or Not To Eat

Many areas have restrictions on how much fish from local waters is safe to eat. Because stripers swim up and down the coast as well as through rivers and bays, there is a good chance they will at one time or another come into contact with stuff that is bad for you. As an example, there are warnings about eating fish from the upper Delaware Bay and Delaware River. Stripers do move to that area in the spring and some stay around all year. So how do we decide if they are safe to eat? I would not make a steady diet of fish that live all year in this area or in the lower Hudson River or any other highly industrialized environment. I grew up on the banks of the Delaware River, and it has seen some pretty bad treatment.

On the other hand, I would and do eat stripers that I have caught in cleaner areas. How much of the bad stuff they retain from their time in contaminated areas, I don't know, and neither does anyone else. Most of the pollutants wind up in the striper's fat and skin. I remove the skin and the dark meat down the side before cooking, so that should reduce the risk. At least once a week, I eat fish that I have caught, and I have made it to my 63rd birthday. I may die tomorrow, but I don't think it will be from eating fish.

Index

Page numbers in italics indicate illustrations.